God
Doesn't Waste
A Hurt

A Life of Abuse to
A Story of Redemption

GYASMIN E. MATOS

WESTBOW
PRESS®
A DIVISION OF THOMAS NELSON
& ZONDERVAN

WestBow Press books may be ordered through booksellers or by contacting:

WestBow Press
A Division of Thomas Nelson & Zondervan
1663 Liberty Drive
Bloomington, IN 47403
www.westbowpress.com
844-714-3454

ISBN: 978-1-6642-7375-7 (sc)
ISBN: 978-1-6642-7376-4 (hc)
ISBN: 978-1-6642-7377-1 (e)

Library of Congress Control Number: 2022913786

Print information available on the last page.

WestBow Press rev. date: 04/26/2023

Contents

Dedication

I dedicate this book to my precious mother. I look forward to seeing you on the other side in the future for eternity. It is my hope that you are smiling down from Heaven rejoicing that I am finally doing what I was called to in this life – caring for seniors and helping others through my writings. Here is to you, Mamacita!

Introduction

Please note that all names have been changed to protect the identity and privacy of the people involved and I am also writing under a Pen Name. My autobiography has been written to share with the many women who are, (or have been), in my shoes. Living in silence when one is abused is life altering.

Existing in these dynamics hindered how I viewed myself, life, and relationships. Out of my own dysfunction, I would continue to stop the process of my healing by returning to relationships that were unhealthy. This only delayed my growth process keeping me stuck and not knowing how to become free, but I desperately wanted to be.

To the best of my ability I loved God and through my pain, I learned how to draw near to Him. Many hard lessons were learned with just Him and I. Going to others for help often times left me feeling very misunderstood. Until someone has walked in the shoes of an abused person, they may not have the ability to comprehend the reality of what it entails.

My healing recovery has taken a lot of hard work and the process started with crying out to God for help in peeling back the layers of my own pain. In order for me to achieve that, I had to stop living in denial about it. It hindered me from having effective communication with my family and others that came into my circle of influence.

My relationships with men usually had some form of dysfunction that included Partner Betrayal Trauma, (PBT), Sexual Addictions, (SA), and Intimacy Anorexia, (IA). This then caused me to experience Post Traumatic Stress Disorder, (PTSD), Obsessive Compulsive Disorder, (OCD), and Broken Heart Syndrome, (BHS), which made the quality of my life very poor for a very long time.

I battled with fibromyalgia, rheumatoid arthritis, adrenal fatigue, depression, anxiety, cancerous cysts, suicidal thoughts, along with high blood pressure and cholesterol. I had suppressed much of my past and later learned that I was also subjected to Satanic Ritual Abuse, (SRA), as a child.

Not knowing that I was never created to be treated this way kept me very ill throughout the years. The onset of my conditions all stemmed from rejection and the lack of security I did not have throughout my life. Then there were the abusive relationships with men and others that played into much of the trauma I endured. Many of the women in my family line had also lost themselves in the vicious cycle of abuse. It was their way of living and they accepted it without seeking help from others. To do so was taboo.

As a child, this caused me not to believe that I could have anything better in my life. I was programmed to settle for less in many of my relationships and I learned to not have a voice on certain things. I existed in an atmosphere of being controlled, which left me in fear, doubt, and trauma most of the time.

For me, this resulted in five marriages and divorces to the same type of man with different faces that I will share about later on in my book. Each one had some form of abusiveness, which left a trail of suffering for everyone that came into their lives. As I began to learn about the world of abuse, I could clearly see that satan tries nothing new. He uses the similar tactics masked in different, people, places, and circumstances.

This is why the same vicious cycle kept reoccurring within my family circle. The patterns of being rejected, taken advantage of, living in domestic violence, and being abandoned was a generational curse that ran through our families. Many of us turned into wounded grown adults scarred by our past hurts, who then passed it down to our children.

I grew up being so love-starved that I went looking for it in all the wrong places. I believe that there are many women who have this same story and it is not being told. When I began to get healthy, I chose to stop the cycle of doing the same thing expecting different results. I became determined that this dysfunctional way of living would stop with me and I continued seeking the answers that only God could give.

Throughout my years of recovery, I learned that the lifelines to my sanity were pressing into God through deep prayer, seeking professional and spiritual help, along with educating myself in the areas I was struggling with. There was lots of journaling, learning to understand my trauma dreams, and much soul searching. My background in healthcare trained me to look beyond the surface of things and I had to apply it to my own Healing Journey.

I asked God to lead me to the right individuals for my recovery and He did. I also had my inner circle of various Therapists, Coaches, Mentors, Prayer Partners, Support Groups, and friends helping me. The illnesses I dealt with were not all psychological either, but also consisted of demonic oppression, due to living a life that was very bleak for so many years.

I never really knew what happiness was and I when I did try to find it, I was only left disappointed. I also died physically, emotionally, financially, and spiritually several times only to be resurrected by a God. He just would not let me die, despite the many times I wanted to. I was plagued with a heaviness of never feeling like I was enough and that I was unworthy.

All of this kept me from pursuing my writing career, until now. The words you will read are from a never-ending journey of putting my life on paper. I can finally say that I accomplished the greatest task ever – telling my Life Story.

As you read on, maybe you will see yourself through the pages of this book. Our lives can help others, if we will be willing to be transparent, take off the mask of everything being okay, and trust that, *"God doesn't waste a hurt."*

1

How It All Began

I was born in New York and came out to California when I was 5-years old. I remember seeing pictures of my family and how cute we all were in our little outfits. My mother loved fashion and enjoyed having us be well dressed when we were out and about doing life. However, if we got dirty or needed to use the bathroom, Lord help us!

I usually had a cute dress on that my mother would make herself, along with colored tights, long pick tails, and stylish shoes to match. I remember seeing one picture of my brother around 4-years old in a three-piece suit with the cutest gangster hat and shoes that looked like a pair of Stacey Adams. He stood beside our gorgeous mother, as she held his hand smiling down at him lovingly.

While we looked like a happy and well off family, our lives were far from being normal. My father and my mother both enjoyed telling stories of our pasts to others, but they were not telling the real story that was taking place behind closed doors. None of us knew what was true and was a lie, as we got caught up in the stories they would tell. Somehow, our abuse became a figment of our imaginations.

All of my life, I grew up hearing about my miraculous birth from my mother and she would tell it to anyone who would listen. It always went something like this and in her Hispanic accent to go along with it, *"One night, I was trying to sleep, I began to have lots of pain inside of me.*

I knew something was wrong and I tried to get Gyasmin's father to wake up and take me to the hospital, but he would not.

He said I was not far along enough to be giving birth yet, but I knew something was wrong. I put my hands on my stomach and began to pray to God to touch me and keep my baby safe. The pain was so strong, but then a miracle happened! I saw God's big hands come down from Heaven, go inside my stomach, and cover my Gyasmin. At that moment the pain stopped and I felt a peace."

My mother always swore that I was her, *"miracle child,"* born specifically to take care of her. I grew to believe that it was so as well, because from the ages of 14 to 55, I was my mother's Care Giver, until she passed. What really happened that night was my dad was heavily intoxicated and told my mother to be quiet, she was over reacting, and to go to sleep. It was then that the spirit of rejection entered me before I was even born, but I do believe that mother's encounter with God saving me was real.

The Early Years

As I grew up, memories of my childhood faded and I cannot remember much of my past like others do. In studying the effects of trauma to a person, I learned that I had blocked out various periods of my life. I eventually began to have flash backs, which led me to question things more.

I distinctly remember one repeated dream I had that made no sense to me. I was a toddler running down the hallway of our old family home when I would fall to the floor in front of my brother's bedroom door. The scene would then shift and I would be in a man's arms in front of a window. The whole room was pitch black and I was about 4-years old. I do remember not feeling safe with this man and knew that something was wrong, but then the dream would end. It would always leave me wondering what it was all about, especially with how uncomfortable I would feel when I awoke.

One afternoon, I was looking out my kitchen window while doing dishes and I was in my mid-20s. Suddenly, I had a flash back of a man's face come before me and I knew it was the man in my dream. I then though about a family member staying with us at one time when I was a child. I later asked my mother and sister more about who he was and things started making sense to me about this particular dream. This man had come to live temporarily with our family. During that time, he *molested* me and I had blocked it out for years.

Due to it being so much for my little mind to process back then, this trauma was now coming up in my dreams. As I processed through it more, I began to recall numerous men who had been in and out of my life from childhood up to my teen years. More memories began to surface and the piecing together of my past was beginning.

One of those times was when I was 13-years old and I had an argument with my mother. As I would occasionally do, I went to work with her that day. After we fought, I stomped out of her place of employment and began to walk home alone. I was not prepared for what was to come either. A man driving an old car pulled up beside me and asked me if I wanted a ride. As I turned towards the vehicle looking into the passenger side window, I saw that he had no pants on and was fondling himself.

The look on his face was full of lust and I quickly ran home fearing he would follow me. Talk about stress, trauma, and anxiety! Trying to comprehend what I had just saw was not something I could do and I was completely terrified. I had never actually *seen* a man naked before either.

When I got home, I saw my father and I wanted to tell him what I had just experienced, so I could feel comforted and protected. Yet, I knew deep down inside I could never be that vulnerable with him. How could I tell him what I saw? How could I say to him how insecure and scared I was? How could I ever feel safe with a Dad who did not know how to care for and protect me?

I did not understand then that this man had just sexually violated me by exposing himself, causing me to see what I never should have seen. I blamed myself for getting mad at my mother, leaving as I did, and that this was my punishment for doing so. The worst part was that I could not bring myself to tell my parents about it. That was my life though back then – me stuffing my emotions and living in the denial of my pain.

The Family

When I was 10-years old, my parents divorced and life became even more of a nightmare leaving me feeling helpless. With my mother now being a single parent and working so much, my siblings were fighting frequently. As teenagers, they were going through a lot already, along with seeing our parents split up.

In watching how they treated each other, I saw that they were no different from my mother and father in how they fought. Fear gripped me at a very young age when I would hear voices raise, cursing, and physical abuse start. There were merciless fights that took place where they were acting out on the rage they had within them towards one another. They could not take it out on our parents, so it came out against one another. We all had so many unanswered questions and insecurities from the abuse we had been exposed to in our home.

Once my siblings would start to argue, they became unstoppable. As the youngest, all I could do was cry, scream for them to stop, and sometimes I would get caught in the middle. Sadly, they were only repeating what our parents had modeled for us.

We each had our own set of addictions to numb the pain that came in the form of drugs, alcohol, being overly controlling, manipulative, narcissistic, compulsive overeating, (or not eating), and buying things we could not afford to validate who we were. We all began smoking at a young age and that addiction stayed with each of us for many years to come. These areas were how we coped with the life we had. I remember thinking, *"I never asked to be born, so why am I here stuck in this mess?"*

The marks of the life I was born into left many triggers within me. When I had witnessed how the men in our family would fight with an intent to harm someone, I learned that men were not safe. To see how they treated the women in our family only bred a strong resentment towards them. There was so much dysfunction that I would walk on egg shells most of the time. It also taught me to become a rescuer and an enabler just to keep the peace. This turned into having co-dependent tendencies in most of my relationships as well.

Due to my parent's divorce and what my mother went through, I did not have the ability to be a child and I grew up quickly. At 14-years old,

I was running the whole house, paying the bills, cooking, and cleaning. My siblings were long gone living their own lives, but not me. I could not leave our mother, because I saw how much pain she was carrying.

However, I dealt with being overly protective, controlled, and manipulated to keep me in check. It is how she was raised and it was all she knew. Growing up in this atmosphere brought me much heartache and suppressed anger with no real outlet. Due to my mother's ways, I was the only one who had a close relationship with her out of all the family.

The reality of this hurts and my siblings have their own set of issues towards our parents till this very day. In their own ways, they did try to help my mother, but she was too lost in her own pain that none of them could tolerate her in their lives for very long. I have always said that, *"Children are what they live with,"* and each one of us had become like our parents.

We were affected by the dysfunctional ways we lived in and I can only image how my parents must have felt. In their time, counseling was unheard of and pride reigned in them heavily that would never admit it was needed. Sadly, my mother never fully recovered from the divorce to our father either.

As I saw what was happening and how depressed she was, I ached with, (and for), her. That imprint of trauma began to take root within me forming the lie that this way of life was, *"normal."* The sad part was that my father stopped coming around to see us shortly after the divorce and that left a gaping hole in all of his children's hearts.

The Teen Years

After my parents divorced, growing up required my mother to work long hours to support me and my siblings and we became latchkey kids. I learned to be an adult before I even knew what it was to be a child. Being left alone brought many problems within the home and when were not in school, our instructions were not to go outside.

I became overly responsible, because I did not want to add more strain to an already stressful household. In do this, a very unhealthy connection developed between my mother and I. Seeing the pain she went through with my family and the struggles she had in trying to find herself when our father left was not easy. Without even knowing what was happening, I became the mother and she became the child.

My mother had only received a third grade education and she was trained to sew as a teenager. In her teens, she married my father and stayed with him for 18-years. Divorce had given her the responsibility to raise three kids on her own now. There were nights when I would lay in her arms and see her weeping silently.

I remember us rubbing each other's arms or hands to bring comfort to one another. We each suffered silently and in different ways, but we understood each other without saying a word. That stayed in our relationship up until the day she passed in 2019. I loved touching her hands and seeing them cover mine. It was a sign of our unity and that we would be okay, as long as we had each other.

As I grew, I had an increasing rage within me that I did not understand. I remember times when I would sit in a corner and scream from the top of my lungs, because I was so furious inside. I can see now that it was my way of releasing my pain, which also contributed to me taking my anger out on certain people in school.

Children with many soul wounds do not know on how to manage their emotions and I was one of them. This produces much rebellion, anger, violence, disrespect to others, and acting out in ways that only bring harm. I had my moments in experimenting with drugs, alcohol, ditching school with friends, but even then, I was the, *"responsible,"* one in the crowds I associated with.

I also was bullied in high school, so I chose to become friends with those who could not defend themselves to protect them from being harassed. I would spend some of my afternoons in the library studying or being tutored by my friends. I worked in the School's Attendance Office as well, which helped develop my love for working in Office Administration. I went on to take Secretarial, Shorthand, and Computer Classes later on.

Yet, I still longed for the love of my father and I began to seek attention from boys in all the wrong ways. I wanted to be accepted, but I did not know the difference between being, *"loved"* and being, *"used."*

My teen years continued with becoming more overly responsible in caring for others, especially my mother. I did not experience the joy of dating or falling in love, causing me not to develop emotionally.

Fear and guilt were so prevalent in my life that it stifled me in various ways. In becoming a Caretaker so young, it shaped my way of thinking to be an over achiever. I felt I had to, *"fix"* people and things, which only enabled others to take advantage of me. What transpired in my teens kept a little girl inside a young woman's body desperately trying to find my way out.

I was filled with shame, misconceptions, regret, self-doubt, and an underlining resentment that I did not know how to manage. I struggled with what love was and battled low self-esteem, which only added to weight problems later on. As I dealt with constantly feeling not good enough, food became my comfort and I remember where my food addiction began.

It was the summer of 1977 and my older sister and I went to visit our father for a few weeks. He continued to work a lot and I distinctly recall there was much eating going on to fill the void of him not being there. When I returned home from that trip, I was 20 pounds heavier. I also came back feeling even more rejected by our father and very confused about myself. I kept thinking why he could not love me back the way I needed to be.

At such a young age and feelings so unloved, it caused me to begin allowing boys to treat me disrespectfully becoming their target of amusement. To make matters worse, I was exposed to pornography at that time also and it tarnished my already unstable view of intimacy between a man and a woman. I had no clue what a healthy relationship was and no one in my life that remotely resembled anything Godly.

My first date took place on my 16th birthday and it was with someone I was not very interested in, nor do I remember what we did. I even saw my first date much later on in life while I was shopping, but he did not see me. Instantly, a deep sadness filled my soul, along with the disappointment I felt about something that should have been a great memory not being so. Until that very moment, I did not realize how traumatized I was by it all.

As I continued on in me teenage years, a desperate need for attention began surfacing more. I would find myself in relationships with school boys who would do degrading things to me and I was mortified. I even stopped going to any dances or school activities and distanced myself from getting too close to anyone. Little did I know that this way of being would carry over into my adult years.

As An Adult

I learned that every situation I have been in has a *purpose* for it. The process of unraveling things within me to get me to the other side of things has become a never-ending journey. I have learned that quick fixes was not the path the God would let me take. My choices in relationships were based on things I had seen growing up. This was not a good platform for me to build anything upon. I also felt that my looks were what defined me, along with what I did for a living.

All I knew is that I enjoyed working in Office Administration, had a desire to write, and was definitely a Type A personality. If my name was going to be on it, my work had to be perfect. At least my work would be right, despite everything else in my life not being so. I was usually dealing with one thing or another and tried my best to hide it from everyone.

Working in Corporate America caused me to become hard and numb all at the same time. The office politics were always there and I had the issues at home to face, along with caring for my mother. It was like I was on auto-pilot in those years just to survive. My life felt like one big roller coaster of twists and turns. Sadly, there was abuse taking place at work *and* home. It taught me to be tough and not show too much emotion.

It is a wonder how I made it on somedays, as I would work myself to exhaustion, come home to take care of the family, go to bed, and rise early the next morning to do it all over again. If I was married, there was usually some form of marital discord with my mate. I felt like I was on an emotional roller coaster constantly. One day I was fine and the next day I was all over the place.

That all changed for me in 2010 when I left working in Administration and began caring for my mother full-time after she had major back surgery. I became more caring and sensitive to things and people in those days. I started to get in tune with myself and I had such a love for God. My desire was to have a better life than what I was living and to give my mother better care than she was receiving. Due to so much personal tragedy, I had developed a sensitivity to others pain. This led me to becoming an, *"Empath,"* as some would call me.

However, the black outs of my past were catching up with me and I wanted the emptiness within to be gone. I had no clue where to begin to change and I was too busy taking care of everyone else, but me. I realized this when I was strolling with my mother throughout her Senior Citizen Apartment complex one day.

She loved to see everyone's garden while she walked her dog, along with having small talk with the neighbors. The conversations were usually the same – how they are enduring through their life struggles. Then it hit me – I had become my mother – my life was filled with nothing by challenges and I was just, *"surviving."*

2

Trying to Fill the Void

I WAS AROUND 3-YEARS OLD WHEN MY PARENTS HAD A VERY INTENSE fight. As I write this, I am envisioning the scene that took place long ago. My siblings and I were all huddled in the middle of my parent's bed and our mother was crying uncontrollably. Her mascara was running all down her face and outside the bedroom door our father was packing up to leave *again*. I have only a few other memories of other times like this.

I distinctly remember another incident also of abuse where I was less than 5-years old and my parents had another serious argument. My mother would take long drives to calm her nerves and I usually went with her. At a young age, I quickly learned that when she was upset, I could make her feel better by *singing*.

This particular time she was weeping, along with gripping the steering wheel very tightly. She could barely see through the tears that kept streaming down her face let alone be able to drive straight. In seeing the car swerve to the left and right of the road, I was scared for her and myself.

Yet, all I knew is that Mommy was hurt and I needed to do something, so I would sing my little heart out. I would sing anything that came into my mind and kept on singing the whole time she was driving. All I remember is seeing her smile and I felt good that she did.

Although I did not understand it, I sensed her pain. Even at that young age, my heart was sensitive to abuse and trauma.

It was also then that I started trying to fill the void of my mother's unhappiness. I became her, *"shadow,"* in everything she did and remained there, until the day she died. The imprint of trying to make things better for her became the pattern that we would walk in throughout our lives together.

Unfortunately, I also transferred trying to make everything okay over into my romantic relationships. With no healthy male role models to learn from, I would try to fix the wounded men that I attracted out of my own brokenness and need to be feel wanted. As I have healed in this area, I now know that I seeking the love I needed from my father. I did not comprehend what healthy love looked like. This resulted in my view of relationships and marriage being based on what I saw growing up in my family.

In one way or another, each of my relationships consisted of living in a toxic atmosphere and the effects of it remained at work within me throughout the years. Up until my 50s, I was a woman who had been rejected, abused, neglected, abandoned, and misunderstood multiple times by others. Even as a Godly woman, I did not know who I was created to be. There were so many mixed messages from my upbringing and misunderstandings of what the scriptures *actually* said about being subjected to abuse. I had a heart for God and His word, but I needed so much soul healing.

In the midst of it all, there were things that God had gifted me to do. I definitely had the talents for working in Administration, but was laid-off twice within a few years. That is when I decided to become an Independent Contractor and open my own business. I was tired of the office politics and insecurity of the job market, especially after the 9/11 tragedy in New York.

It affected me greatly and even though I appeared to be strong on the outside, I felt like I did not fit in anywhere on the inside. There was much labeling, being misunderstood, and judging by the females. I was a, *"no nonsense,"* type of woman, who did her job well. The Executives whom I did work for embraced me as being their, *"Office Wifey,"* so to speak. Sometimes I knew more about them than their own wives in working the long hours we did together. Thankfully, no affairs took place although some of them sure wanted to have one with me!

I did long for a relationship with a man who could love me past my pain though. I had to learn that what I expected or wanted out of others was not something I would ever fully get. My idealism in this area was a hard lesson to learn. It has taken me on an interesting path in discovering who I am and what, *"healthy love,"* is and what it is not.

Eventually, I also saw that I was the common denominator in all of my failed relationships. This caused me to begin seeking out *why* I continued choosing dysfunctional men throughout my life. It usually caused me to end up in the same situation I swore I would never put myself in again. I was definitely blinded to my dilemma and pride ruled heavily within me, because of my deep insecurity. Bottom line – it all stemmed from my soul wounds.

My, *"Man Picker,"* was definitely broken and I had not observed the way God calls a man to treat a woman and vice versa. I finally began to admit that I needed help to change from the inside out. My soul wounds were too deep and not only in me, but in my family.

Through my shattered heart and mindsets, the enemy had several open doors with demonic influences all around me. Each relationship I had been in left a trail of brokenness and it was a challenge to allow God to go into my inner parts for my healing.

Learning how to re-parent myself in Him was a tall order for me. It was like Nicodemus asking Jesus on how a person could be born again in the Book of John. When the process finally did begin, it took me on a very long journey – one that not only changed my life, but others also.

The Day My Father Left

After 18-years of my parents living in an abusive marriage, they divorced and my father left our family permanently. I was 10-years old and life was never the same, as I knew it to be. It was then that I really began to see men differently. I viewed them as people who were not to be *trusted*. I felt alone and abandoned on so many levels by my father.

As a child, having an insignificant and uncared for mentality crept into me, but I never once dare voice my pain to my father. The fear of being rejected even more by having my feelings minimized would not let me do so. It was not until my latter 50s and my mother's passing that I was able to finally bring myself to share my heart with him through a letter I was led to write. Sadly, he never responded either.

Deep inside, I longed to be loved by him and eventually had to grieve that was not going to happen. I would learn to accept that my father could not give me what he did not have in him. It is how he was raised and from the stories I could remember, my grandparents were not the most loving people. I also never personally met them from either side of my parent's families.

Then there was the anger my Mom carried towards my father that our family would hear when she spoke of him. I realize now that my mother did what countless women do in not managing their pain well. She had no clue how to manage her emotions and it was internalized allowing it to feaster into unforgiveness. With that came being domineering, controlling, and manipulative with an undercurrent of rage as she suffered inside. She did not know what peace was and lived in fear continually.

I was the youngest of three children. My sister was the oldest and suffered a lot of abuse from all the rage that existed in both of our parents. My brother and father carried their own set of heart issues that made them the men they were and are still today.

Resentment, bitterness, and insecurity oozed out of our family in so many areas. It turned our home into a place where we felt like we were near a time bomb that would explode at any given moment. When our father left, it sent a loud and negative message to all of us that shaped our perspectives on life, love, marriage, and parenting.

Until later, I was not able to understand how God called a man and woman to be in a marriage. I saw marriage as an, *"obligation,"* and never realized how love starved our whole family was. My parent's divorce was a bitter one and full of much betrayal. I never understood how two people could do such harm to one another after claiming they loved each other once.

Looking for Love in All the Wrong Places

There was a repeated pattern in my life of choosing men that I saw, *"potential."* I became involved with the same type of abusive people continually, but they were with different faces and names each time. Every relationship had the characteristics of either my parents or siblings – they were filled with deep insecurity and a lack of empathy for others. The programming of abuse had taken root in their souls and I was just like them in my earlier years.

As I began to reflect on how each relationship impacted me differently, I was baffled by how I could be so smart in other areas and so naïve in my love life. Due to this, I carried a lot of shame and blame towards myself as why I would do this. I found it was hard to forgive myself and move on from my past. I felt that it was an endless cycle of poor choices and repeated dysfunction patterns, but did not understand why.

I would work long hours to keep myself busy, along with compulsive shopping sprees, eating, and getting involved with men out of my loneliness. This was my normal way of living and a generational curse that I learned about later on. Pretty much all the women in our family were with the wrong man and this would happen to me every time I would begin to get healthy.

Satan sure did have an executed plan and he was working it masterfully for a very long time. From my birth into my teen years, I could not express anger. I had seen the repercussions of it from the abuse within my family. My childhood was filled with blocking out moments of feeling helpless, which broke me down even more.

Due to feeling powerlessness, I was also one who fought for those who were bullied. I would go to their rescue and wished that someone would do the same for me. I ended up making an inner vow that when I got older, *no one* would push me around. Inner vows like that have a way of deeply gripping one's heart and soul. It is like a spider web forming within and the black widow of fear is being spun within a person crippling them.

Just to be accepted, I would often try to buy friendships with gifts, going over and above the call of duty to help others, and working so hard that I had no time for my own family or self-care. I was happy for a while, but it did not last long. When I could not continue winning other's approval, I soon saw that many of my, *"friends,"* really were not friends at all.

I lavished men with gifts and constant attention in order for them not to, *"forget me."* This only attracted men to me that would leech off of women. Things would be wonderful in the beginning, but it did not last for long before the abuse would start. When I began to have needs and wants, I was told that I was being selfish. It was then that I realized I was being taken for granted. When my desire for attention was not reciprocated and I stopped giving them all they wanted, one of us would end the relationship.

I dealt with a lot of guilt for marrying each one of my husbands, (more on that later). Even though I saw the relationships were unhealthy, I was too unhealthy to see that *I was* putting them before God. I was equating the love of God to that of a man. It was the void I had left in me from the lack of love by my father.

If I crossed the line with a man, I had a view of not being worthy enough to approach God and felt like I had to then get married. This is where the multiple divorces came in later. I also stayed in abusive situations, because I was counseled by some church leadership that, *"God hates divorce."* This only added to my disgrace of not measuring up to His standards.

It led me to believe that I had to earn God's approval, along with those that claimed to love me. I was driven to be thinner, stronger, and perfect in all I did to be accepted. The problem was, I never could, (or would), be able to.

All the men in my life had some sort of injustice done to them also. This caused them to struggle with their own unresolved conflicts, which led them to being abusive or addicts. I refer to these types of behaviors as, *"addict/abuser."* These men would believe the same lie that I had been told in not measuring up and they did not know how to change that lie without help. This only caused them to do to me what was done to them and they knew no other way to do life, unless they chose to get healthy.

I had to learn how to detect these type of wounded men who were waiting to just be given the opportunity to enter my life. I was consumed by them through fear, manipulation, control, and so many other things. This contributed to me losing myself and staying in a vicious cycle of trauma.

Physical Abuse Enters My World

Throughout my teen years, I was involved with various boys. At 16, a friend introduced me to a 30-year old man that would physically abuse me later. I was in a very vulnerable place, as I had just ended a relationship with my one of my high school boyfriends. The pain I was in caused me to seek male companionship and attention. The motto between me and my best friend back then was, *"The best way to fall out of love is to quickly fall in love with someone else."*

This older man caught my attention in many areas – his age, he had been married before, had twin boys, we were both from the same ethnic group, and the fact that he gave me attention was alluring. As a teenager, I thought it was a privilege to have such an, *"older and experienced man,"* interested in me. As we began to get to know each other, I saw him struggle to keep his life together. He was not stable where he lived, had issues with his former wife, and had an estranged relationship from his children and family.

Ultimately, I found myself rescuing him. He charmed his way into my mother's heart also. She even allowed him to live in our downstairs basement that had a private entryway. As the time went by, I slowly began to give up my school friends to be with him. I was not even able to participate in my High School Prom, because he could not attend with me. What should have been a memorable night became a regret later on for me, as every teenager should have the joy of attending their prom.

The first time he hit me was so unexpected and shocking all at the same time. I was with my best friend and her boyfriend. We went on a double date, which involved drinking and smoking marijuana, along with a drive through a park. We decided to stop at a certain spot, but my friends stayed in the car. This man and I went out to sit on a nearby bench to talk.

As we did, somehow a fight started between us and I cannot even remember why. Before I knew it, he had punched me in the face with his full fist. My friends did not even have the decency to come to my aid either and the rest of the night was a blur. What I do recall is the next morning awaking and feeling my face bruised and I had a severe headache. I was shocked at what I saw when I looked in the mirror. My face was black and blue, along with being swollen in different places. Until my mother went to work, I literally hid in my room, so she would not see me.

As I tried to recall what happened, I began to shake and my memory was foggy. I could only put bits and pieces together and when I did, I went numb inside on the reality of what I had just endured. I had seen years of abuse in my own family and vowed that I would not let it happen to me. It traumatized me to see this repeated pattern now taking place in my own life. The worst part was it would be just the beginning of many more beatings to come.

I did finally break free from the relationship for a while and life went on, (or so I thought it would), but he would not let me go. This pattern repeated itself throughout our entire time together and the abuse lasted for 10-years. In that time, I was stalked, beaten, raped, and abandoned by him over and over.

As the years went on, this man turned to cocaine to sooth his own pain. I did not realize that he had lost his way long before I came into the picture. He only shared with me what he wanted me to know about his past. I would later come to learn that there were some deep hidden wounds that he was carrying.

At 17, I became a Christian and I tried to get him to go to church with me. He did at times, but he would return to his addictions and way of abusing me. Then one day he just disappeared. After years had gone by, I received a phone call and it was *him*. The voice on the other line was different though. I listened to what he had to say and then hung up the phone in awe. He had called to ask for my forgiveness, because of all the abuse he had put me through.

He had finally put his life in order and wanted to thank me for introducing him to God. He shared that he was still in love with me and wanted to see me again, but I was already engaged to be married to someone else. That day, I finally got the closure I needed by truly saying goodbye to the man who took 10-years of my life and it did something within me.

I wondered how God could use me to lead someone to Christ in the midst of my abuse. I tolerated so much from him, because I desperately wanted him to love me back. From that day on, I never heard from him again and my life continued. Sadly, I regretted our time together, because it was through him that physical abuse entered my world. Being with him caused me to emotionally die more than I already had. My reality was that I had become my mother and I was crippled by it all.

My Healing Journey

By the time I was finally able to wrap my mind around what my life was and allow myself to acknowledge it, many years had passed me by. A bleeding and very broken heart from all my failed relationships I had been in left me deeply marked. Even after walking with the Lord since I was 17-years old, I did not comprehend the love of Christ and who He was fully. I held an unspoken belief that God could love everyone else, *but me.*

I toiled between addictions to food, cigarettes, and chronic depression. I use to say that, *"The days I looked my best, are the days I felt the worst inside."* I had masked my pain by looking all together on the outside, while I was falling apart on the inside. Later on, I began to understand the dynamics of being co-dependent, having Obsessive Compulsive Disorder, (OCD), Post Traumatic Stress Disorder, (PTSD), Irritable Bowel Syndrome, (IBS), and Fibromyalgia.

Then there was the stress and anxiety, along with high blood pressure and cholesterol that I had have to face. I tried to overcome by educating myself about all the psychological theories in what I thought was wrong with me. Yet, I was still stuck in fighting an inability to enjoy life long-term.

I had a desire to support others who were walking in the shoes I had walked in. I empathized with them to the point of becoming enraged *for them.* My buttons were definitely pushed when I would see women and children being abused, disrespected, or abandoned. I did not want them to go through what I had and felt a call to help, but I knew I had to get help for myself first.

My story was the typical one of many women who are abused, isolated, confused, weak, and lost, along with being financially and mentally unstable. I learned to accept that I needed someone who could pin point the problems I faced and work through them with me. It would take time and it did not always happen with one Counselor or Therapist.

I did not know how or who I could trust, so embracing just anyone was very hard for me. I would need a village of people to walk me through my pain. My ability to even trust myself was foreign to me and the task to bring me back to who God created me to be would become a full-time way of life.

In my quest to learn, I went through several types of programs with a library of Christian books on love, life, abuse, marital issues, self-help, co-dependency, addictions, and healing from past hurts. I was fascinated with the heart of women, marriage, becoming healthy, and learning how to heal in the midst of my own traumas, tragedies, and abandonments. It became my life passion to help others the way I needed to be helped.

Many have labeled me various things, but I have learned about *who God says I am*, thankfully. Knowing this eventually turned my life around, but not until I went through more than one marriage and divorce. During these times, I was so lost that seeing a light at the end of the tunnel became very challenging for me.

Seeking and trying to be loved was all I knew to do, but in all the wrong places and with unsafe individuals. As I look back now, I can see that God was always there keeping me from fully destroying myself. His interventions would come through a person reaching out to me or a message I would hear to keep my hope going, as I got so sick and tired of being sick and tired. This caused me to want to end my suffering by no longer living.

It has been a never-ending journey to survive and I definitely have been sustained by His mercy and grace. Thankfully, on Easter of 2020, I relinquished my right to hold on to anything that caused me to be, *"bitter and not better."* I was taken into a deeper journey of finding out more about God's love for me, how I fit into all I was created to be, and in dealing with letting go of my right to be right.

For years, I felt that I had justification for what I carried in my heart towards my past. However, a continual shift has been taking place that is helping me to get to the other side of the pain that has held me bound for so long. It did not come quickly either and even now as I write this, I am faced with things I wish I would not have to deal with. Yet, I continue to believe that God is faithful in spite of it all.

3

Satanic Ritual Abuse, (SRA)

IT WAS A TYPICAL EVENING WHERE I ENTERED INTO A DARK NIGHTMARE after falling asleep. I had dealt with dreams a majority of my life, but this one was different. It was as if God was awakening a part of me that no longer could stay suppressed. I had been studying on Biblical Dream Interpretation and seeking help from those who understood this more than I did.

In this dream, I saw myself buried alive in a coffin and I was about 8-years of age. I became claustrophobic, panicking, and gasping for air. I tried to stay calm by breathing slowly, but the feelings of suffocating were consuming me. I was in pure darkness and I abruptly awoke in a cold sweat breathless.

I ended up having this dream one more time and it left me wondering, *"Did this actually happen to me in real life???"* Sadly, I would come to learn that it had. This began my journey into what had been subjected to through satanism.

I did not put too much thought into why I had no recollection of various parts of my childhood. I figured that this was something that I had suppressed, because of all the abuse I had experienced. I never realized that there was much more to it, until the dreams continued to plague me. I also had regular ones of relationships I had been in where I was left abandoned.

My other dreams were of work situations and the office politics that had also traumatized me. Yet, some dreams were so demonic in nature that I would actually have experiences where my body was black and blue when I awoke the next morning. I later learned that I was being ritualistically abused in my sleep. How? Through astro projecting.

This is where I am spiritually taken into the second heavens and there demonic rituals are done. This realm is satan's, just as the third heavens are Gods. I would also find myself feeling like I had done something before, but could not remember it. I later learned that this can happen when someone has endured, *"mind programming."* I was easily triggered by certain words, places, or things where I would go into auto-pilot and be in a trance.

What I was enduring in my waking life was just as real as in my dream world. I had no clue about the vast abuse that the enemy does to our souls and bodies while we are awake and asleep. I encountered times where there was no real rest for me leaving my soul in a brain fog state. I would awake fatigued from the night before or after a nap. The medical field labeled me with all sorts of things.

Through spiritually cleansing my blood line, I would later find out that there was a spirit of infirmity that came in through soul wounds inflicted upon me in my abuse. When I was ritualistically abused in the heavenlies, my sleep was robbed by my dreams causing me bodily pain. My nightmares were like living disasters and I had no clue how to get free.

Thankfully, God sent some divine connections my way to teach me about SRA and, along with on-line communities that help other survivors. Lisa Meister, Author and Podcast Host of *Only God Rescued Me,* was one person that God used to help me heal. God was taking the tragedy of SRA in my life and using it to teach me how the enemy steals, kills, and destroys through sleep and soul trauma.

In turn, God used my awareness of the demonic realm to prepare me for what was to come in the End Times to do more strategic spiritual warfare. All SRA is geared towards doing satan's dirty work in the world leading us right into the anti-Christ coming on the scene. Satan cannot do anything without people that can become embodied by demonic entities.

Many cults even exist through various denominations that can stem from Catholicism, Mormonism, Jehovah Witnesses, Children of

God, Scientology, The Unification Church, Heaven's Gate, and the list could go on. Demonically, they range from Satanism, New Age, Wicca, Santeria, Free Masons, and right up to the Illuminati.

There are also what is known as, *"decoy,"* churches, daycare centers, schools, and universities where hidden ritual abuse and mind programming take place regularly. As you read what I am about to share, you will enter into a world that many do not want to believe even exists, but it does.

SRA Rituals

Satanic rituals consists of animal and human sacrifices, along with brutal and unspeakable torture to people, and especially to children. Gruesome acts of torture take place, such as being put in coffins with snakes, caged up and treated like a dog, bestiality, homosexuality, and so much more. These rituals involve drinking and eating despicable things that cause children to disassociate.

Through SRA torture, a disconnection from ones thoughts, feelings, memories, and surroundings occurs in a person's mind. It affects their sense of identity and life purpose leaving an open door to the spirits of mental illness.

There are women who will become pregnant to Jane and John Doe babies only to give birth to them to be sacrificed to satan at various times throughout the year. There is a satanic calendar that his followers go by and what takes place entails witchcraft, brutality, murder, sex, rape, cruelty, and the cannibalism.

Many that are involved are usually wearing robes with hooded coverings over their heads. A child can actually be raped by over 30 men in one night and there is a heavy use of hallucinogenic drugs, alcohol, and pornography. Some young girls are impregnated by their perpetrators, (which can include family members), and then forced to sacrifice their own children in a ritual.

In 2021, the SRA I had experienced began to surface through generational curses being in full swing and mind control being actively triggered. There were nights where I could feel demons trying to literally take my life by suffocating me in my sleep. Through my own spiritual deliverances, I learned that it was the enemy's mandate not to let the women in my family live in peace, as we had strong warrior spirits for God, so he released a spirit of insanity upon us.

For me personally, I knew too much and was bold enough to tell others. I also love deeply and the demonic realm hates me for that. My heart has become broken with the things that break the heart of God and that made me very dangerous to the demonic world. I became fearless of dying and was ready to for God at any given moment.

I was now a main target for the enemy even more so, but God rose up Spiritual Warriors to wage war on my behalf. I had done so for others all my life and now I was seeing my turn come full circle in being carried through by the remnant of SRA individuals I knew. Then there were the intercessors that He would have pray for me out of the blue. I would get messages from them when I least expected it and it was, *"a word in due season,"* for that particular moment.

I also learned about the stories of others who had been subjected to far darker SRA rituals than I had. There were times where the horrors of my friends were too great for me to digest and I would have to take a step back to process things. My suppressed memories began to show me parts of myself that had been shattered and I entered in specialize therapy for this.

A few individuals came to me for help in coaching them, but I quickly learned that it was not were God was leading me. I stopped doing so and began writing more about the subject to make others aware that it existed. SRA causes a person to have layers upon layers of soul wounds that need to be delicately healed. Taking upon myself the cares of others was not something He released me to do, until I had healed more.

Surviving Satanic Ritual Abuse

In my latter 50s, I was definitely done with the poor quality of my life, which included being sleep deprived. I had suppressed the demonic abuse and programming endured in my childhood from the ages of 10 to 17-years old. As I began to study more on SRA, things started coming back in stages. I recognized that I had been abused by extended family members in the cult called the, "*Santeria.*"

I had vague memories of the rituals they would put me through, but did not realize the extent of it. Getting triggered by babies or animals crying in pain affected me greatly. I later understood that it could have been because I was forced to witness abuse to them in this cult.

My soul had split, (or been shattered), into so many parts just to survive the brutal abuse I experienced. I had developed Multiple Personality Disorder, (MPD), Dissociative Identity Disorder, (DID), Post Traumatic Stress Disorder, (PTSD), Obsessive Compulsive Disorder, (OCD), Irritable Bowel Syndrome, (IBS), and a host of other things.

Through my Spiritual Deliverance, I learned about dividing the soul and spirit, which meant that when a soul wound was created by trauma or SRA, demonic entities would be immediately attached to it. The more trauma I experienced, the more power my perpetrators received from satan. This caused me to disassociate on several levels to avoid the pain, which kept me and my body in a state of pain, confusion, and dysfunction.

I began to study under Dr. Scott Bitcon, who is one of the leading experts on Inner Healing and Deliverance that I have come across. He graciously accepted my request for him to personally walk me through some things as to why I was not being healed. My deliverance was then accelerated from that point on.

Satan wanted to make sure he kept me in destructive and toxic relationships from 19-years of age on. Every time I married and divorced, I became more love starved. There was no connection with the men in my family either, as they were all addict/abusers as well. It is a miracle that I am even sane today.

Reality Check

I was an, "*abuse survivor,*" and I now had a name for it. Coming from this way of life, one thinks that this is how they are to live. The enemy had me so deceived into this way of thinking. I was faced with having to deal with my heart issues and surrender them to God. I began to learn more about praying for others and loving them *from afar*. Reaching out to various people only to be rejected was like having a blistering sun burn and continually being slapped on the back by their dismissal of me. The pain was excruciating and I already had enough to last me a life time.

I usually was the one who initiated things, despite me knowing that the other person probably would not reciprocate. I so longed to be loved, treated with value, respect, and appreciation from my family, others, and the men in my life. I let their validation define me, until God stepped in and gave me some life lessons in, *"living for an audience of One."* Slowly, but surely, He began to deprogram me from the lies the enemy had put in me.

The only person I felt remotely safe with was my mother and she was *gone*. Her home had always been the place where I could go. When she passed away, God miraculously brought in my church family to be by my side. Thankfully, I was able to deal with my past being full of unresolved issues and I toiled with so many unanswered questions.

I had taken an inventory of my life and wanted to make my wrongs right to those I had hurt, offended, or wounded. I wanted to close the door to any legal access the enemy could use against me. Out of my brokenness, I did and said things that hurt a lot of people. The phrase, *"Hurt people, hurt people,"* proved to be true in my world.

I wanted to own the parts I played in my relationships that were in need of much healing, but no one would listen. I was viewed as being who I once was and labeled as such. I could not extend my godly sorrow to them personally, so I wrote letters, sent cards, and e-mails to the individuals God would bring to my heart. I longed to have a restored relationship with them. Yet, no one cared enough to love me back the way I was willing to love them – unconditionally – as God loved me.

In trying to restore my relationships, I realized that one *cannot* give what they do not have. My truth ended up being that I was wanting to receive from others what they did not possess within for themselves let alone others. I had to purpose not to put a round peg into a square whole and I detached completely from all of my family. I went into what I call my, *"Safe Haven,"* to heal. There I learned much in dying to self, how damaged I was, the truths of my emotional insecurities, and so much more.

Those years pushed me into battling for my life, as I became numb from the inside out in what the reality of my world was. I stopped trying to fix everyone and everything around me. I stopped begging others to love me back. I stopped taking the blame for their unforgiveness towards me. I stopped life completely and died to who I once was.

I took a Sabbatical Leave from my coaching to focus solely on writing this book. I did what I never thought I would do – I stopped talking, because no one was listening, but God. I always said to anyone close to me that, *"When I stop talking, that's when you need to be concerned, because I have stopped caring."*

My Safe Haven

For over 3-years after my mother's passing and the final separation from my ex, I went into my cave and rarely came out. I purged my heart and soul like I had never done before and began to address the SRA I had suppressed for years. I studied. I prayed. I wrote. I died over and over again feeling the pain of the millions of blows I had taken. I felt like an Eagle that was sheading its feathers, breaking its own beak off, and becoming so ugly before it comes out to soar in beauty again. I also felt like a caterpillar that was hidden away in a cocoon allowing the metamorphosis process take place and emerge later as a beautifully unique butterfly.

God provided the finances by me working part-time and doing my life coach writing part-time. I went into weekly Therapy and was in some form of Coaching, Mentoring or Study Program daily to help myself heal. I developed a safe on-line community with women as well. Accept for God and the safe people He would bring into my life, I resolved to no longer look to anyone for my validation or purpose in life.

In my Safe Haven, I wanted to learn who I was created to be, where I was going in my life, and how to be all that and more. I finally accepted that I had lived for everyone else in being a people pleaser and now I needed to find out *who I was*. Healing from my wounds and SRA that I had buried deep inside of me was going to be a journey. I accepted the fact that I did not get here overnight and I was not going to get out of where I had been overnight either.

As I continued to stay in my Safe Haven, I began to have many, *"Aha Moments."* God had given me the heart of a Philanthropist with a mandate to be a Publicist for Christ in being a writer. In the years to come, I would begin to walk in my callings and it was all done by the miraculous hand of Papa God, Holy Spirit, and Jesus himself, along with my Guardian Angel, (who never left my side), the Host of Heaven, (which was my Spiritual Army), and the angels that were sent to assist me in achieving all that I was put on this earth to do.

This is a Supernatural outpouring of Godly encounters that not many will understand or even embrace. We are all on a different journey in our lives and have the right to believe, (or not), in this amazing God that loves us so much. In the Prophetic, I grew much there and my God Encounters are very precious to me. I am not on any hallucinogenic drugs either and I have finally begun to see the many prayers that others have said for me coming around.

With several marriages and divorces behind me, I realized that I had been so deceived into believing that I was not enough, I did not deserve better, and I was damaged goods. I was very programmed to believe many lies. I did not break free or even understand what that all meant, until much later. What I was raised in and how that led me to such dysfunctional relationships only set me up to lose. Even as a Christian, there was so much spiritual abuse in the church that I was objectified in who I was there also.

When I started to believe that I did not need to settle for less, could be free from the SRA, and that I was able to deprogram the lies of the enemy, I became someone else. I was re-born into His marvelous light and there was no turning back for me.

4

The Men In My Life

I REMEMBER MY FIRST LOVE GROWING UP AND HIS NAME WAS, "SAM." Oh, how I was smitten with him and his handsome face. As I write this, I can see it right now before me. I was in my teenage years and so longed to be his girlfriend, so when Sam showed interest in me, I was thrilled!

Yet, that would quickly change when I learned that he his heart motives towards me were disingenuous. It was a *bet* he had made with his friends to see if he could get to first base with me. I was crushed, embarrassed, and so broken hearted. Sam would not be the first boy to do this to me either. Sounds like a teenager movie script, huh???

The men in my life have always hurt me. In all of my marital relationships, I had become captive to an addict/abuser, (a person addicted to some form of vice and who abuses others because of it). I saw this happen too many times with the women in our family as well.

Outside of my relationship with Christ, my biggest heart's desire to do is to know what true love is between a man and woman. I long to grow old with a man who will love me like Jesus does where we actually keep our Marriage Vows made on our Wedding Day, *"Till death do us part."*

It is challenging to write this part of my story, but my hope is that whoever reads what I share will glean some wisdom from the mistakes I have made to help them avoid making the same errors. It took me a long time to realize that my past did not have to identify me. I have grown so much through my pain and it has made me sensitive to others who have, (or are), walking in my shoes.

I have been married and divorced five times, (yes, you read it right – five times). Each marriage was full of physical, spiritual, emotional, verbal, sexual, and financial abuse. I have literally been married from the ages of 18 all the way up until 55. It caused me to also carry a lot of shame, until one day I heard Ruth Graham, (Billy Graham's daughter), tell her story. Interestingly, she also experienced being married and divorced more than once – four times to be exact. I then heard Jesus say, *"You are in good company, so drop the shame and trust Me to redeem it all."* What a God we serve!

My first marriage lasted 2-months and the only blessing I received from it was my one and only child. He was a year older than me and a traditional Mexican, who believed a woman was to be home barefoot and pregnant. I later learned that he was an alcoholic, who then left me when I was pregnant with our child for another woman.

He was also the man that date raped me when I was 17 taking my virginity by force. After what took place on that horrible night, we never spoke about it again. In my distorted way of thinking, I felt I *had* to marry him now. I later divorced him after learning of his continued affair with the same woman he left me for the first time. Our child would never know her father and seeing her heart break each time he would not show up for their monthly visits was heart wrenching.

My second marriage lasted 6-years, but we were separated half of the time and he was 10-years older than me. He was a mixture of German and Irish. Throughout our time together, he mercilessly subjected me and our family to domestic violence, which left each of us traumatized beyond words. I finally divorced him when I saw the effects of his physical abuse to my child in back handing her for not doing laundry correctly leaving her with a bloody nose.

I knew that if I would not divorce him for myself to be safe, I would definitely do it for my child to be. I later learned that he had done far worse things to the family. As a mother, it sent me to my emotional grave. Not only did physical abuse reside in our home, but sexual abuse did also and I was not the only one he violated either.

My third marriage was to get out of my second marriage and it lasted 10-years. It turned out to be very abusive, as my ex had severe addictions to pornography, alcohol, and cigarettes. He was 6-years younger than me, Jamaican, and a, *"Mama's Boy."* His mother heavily operated in the spirit of jezebel, along with other family members. She put curses on me and the marriage through witchcraft all in the name of God.

I then learned of an affair he was having on the eve of our 9-year Wedding Anniversary. I finally divorced him almost a year later after he tried to reconcile with me all the while still carrying on an affair with the other woman. He also put me out of our house when she became pregnant with his child and moved her in.

My fourth and fifth marriages were to the *same* man who truly stole a portion of my heart. We were only a few months apart in age and so in infatuated with each other, until I learned of his addictions 5-years into the marriage. He was of a military background and a mixture of Mexican, French, and Indian. He had me so deceived that he was able to see a portion of the, *"the real me,"* which is why he has also been the one man who hurt me and my family the most out of all the rest.

After several years together, we divorced, then remarried, and then divorced again. The issues that prompted us to divorce the first time where never truly addressed, causing the marriage to fail once again. I was not remotely ready for the pain I was entering into with each of these men.

My Man Picker Was Broken

I have always married men with some form of dysfunctional pattern of addictions to being abusive. The reality is that people attract others based on *their* healthiness, (or unhealthiness). When it came to men, satan had planned each one of my destructive relationships to use them against me every time.

It was clear that my ability to pick healthy relationships was fragmented and this only added to not being able to trust myself and others. The unhealthy imprints I lived with were so deeply imbedded into me that I desperately sought to fill the void. How? By looking for love through food, shopping, men, work, and refusing to accept my reality. I longed to feel worthy, loved, appreciated, accepted, adored, and cared for.

With each relationship, I hoped and prayed that things would be different. Despite the abuse continuing, I would still believe the broken promises of men that they would never hurt me again. I lived in a prison within myself and our own homes. Doing life with an addict/abuser makes the atmosphere full of fear, causing a person to feel like they are walking on egg shells all the time.

Each time a relationship would end, it made a deeper hole within my heart. It only caused me to build higher walls of protection. Due to the fear of being betrayed or abandoned again, I grew to not allow myself to be close to anyone for very long. As God's daughter, I had no clue how to embrace His love for me or in seeing Him differently than the earthy men in my life. I felt like I had never really been loved by anyone without them having, *"ulterior motives."* My mindset was so distorted that I could not imagine God could love me either.

Everything in my life was full of control, manipulation, dominance, abuse, and chaos. I survived in Crisis Mode most of the time and knew no other way to live. With each marriage, I tried to change to be what I thought I needed to be for my husbands. Each time I would get into another relationship, I would tell myself, *"This one will be different. I can make him a better person, as I am a good influence on him."* In the end, I eventually learned, (the hard way), that only God can change a person's heart and mind, not me.

Can Being Sexually Violated Exist In Marriage?

I never thought that I would experience such a thing when I was married, *but I did.* I did not even think the term, *"rape,"* could be used in marriage, because if you are married how can you be raped, right? In my second marriage I learned a lot on my Honeymoon night about rape, because that is what happened to me.

The unthinkable of being forced to have sex with my new husband left me in complete and total shock! He had been drinking and a side of him came out that I could see a demonic entity in his eyes. They were full of a hideous evilness that had no mercy. He beat and raped me leaving me like a tossed ragged doll on the floor afterwards. What led to this?

He was in a drunken stupor becoming obsessive and violent, because I did not do something he wanted. I fought hard to have him stop, but it only made him more furious. The blows to my body and face where continuous and then the reality of him forcing himself sexually upon me caused me to go numb. I screamed for help and no one came, despite there being a Police Officer with his wife in the room beside us.

I felt like I was in a dark tormenting dream with no light at the end of the tunnel. That night, I learned that one *can* be raped in marriage. As soon as we returned from the Honeymoon, my intention was to annul the marriage, but addict/abusers do not let go of their victims that easily. I stayed with him out of shear fear, confusion, and manipulation. Despite me having a Restraining Order in place, he would also stalk me and my child. The mind games he played were of him being the predator and me his victim.

Through all of this, I would soon learn what rape was. It is when a person is *forced* to have sex with someone, even your own husband. If it is violent and *against* your will – you are being raped. God never intended any sexual encounter to be that way EVER. What should have been the most exhilarating experience in a couple's life, turned out to be a brutal act of violence against me as a person, woman, and this man's new bride.

I was changed forever from that day forward, which only groomed me to be set-up for the other things that would take place with this man. There were the beatings, drinking, and outbreaks of being locked in a room while he ranted and raged outside the door threatening to kill me. Although I tried to stop him every time he would rape me.

I could not get away from him and he stalked me for 3-years causing me to live in tormenting fear, not to mention what it did to my child, family, and friends. I later learned that he had not only raped and violated me, but he had done it to his children and also to one of my own family members.

I internalized the rapes deep within and did not understand what healthy sexual intimacy was like. I finally divorced him, but it was not in a healthy way. I jumped from the frying pan into the fire with my third marriage that also took me down a whirlwind of abusive paths. These ones were filled with abandonment, rejection, addictions, and deep soul trauma once again.

Addictions and Abuse in My Marriages

My first encounter in dealing with porn addiction was in my latter 30s with my third ex-husband. I was not ready to believe the truth about the secret life he lived. Denial reigned in both of us about the seriousness of his views on intimacy. My, *"woman's intuition,"* was there or really the unction of the Holy Spirit trying to warn me, but I did not listen to it.

I embraced the motto that, *"Boys will be boys,"* and then felt like there was something wrong with me that my ex's would go to porn or infidelity. Each time I learned of sexual unfaithfulness by any of them, I would stay in the marriage, lose weight, and try to compete with the airbrush Porn Stars or the other women they were involved with.

I even saw the imprints of unfaithfulness in my parent's marriage too. The nights where my father would work late, coming home intoxicated, and the terrible fights that took place. My mother knew he was being unfaithful, but what could she do? She had no real education and was at my father's mercy.

In 2019, my precious mother died at 82-years of age from congestive heart failure. On June 1st after putting her down for her afternoon nap, little did each of us know that we had just kissed, hugged, and said our last, *"I love you,"* on this side of heaven. Prior to her passing, she had asked me to not resuscitate her should I find her not breathing. That afternoon, my mother crossed over in her sleep just like she had wanted to.

In mourning her death and what transpired within my marriage at the time, I lost myself. I did not know that I would end up where I was with my ex again. Throughout our years together, there were so many red flags and separations between us that I lost count. I stayed for two reasons: 1) This man was the one that I gave a portion of my heart to; and 2) I did not want to go through another divorce. These were not very good reasons to stay in an abusive marriage. Yet, many women do when they are isolated and being abused behind closed doors. Sadly, I was one of them.

In the time we did have together, there was so much unfaithfulness by him and several addictions within him, along with me being abandoned over and over. I even had a few of the women he had affairs with personally contact me sharing details that ruined me emotionally at that time. One of them had the audacity to harass me a week after my mother's passing.

When I brought it to my ex's attention, he took no responsibility for it. I was still living in my mother's home and he even abandoned me that very night and would not take responsibility for his affair with this woman. Mind you, I had *just* lost my mother, had to be relocated within 30-days, and with nowhere to go.

What did I do? Agreed to reconcile with him and lived to regret it shortly afterwards. Yes, I know, you are all probably shaking your heads going, "Oh, no you did not!!" Yep, I did. That is how ill I was emotionally and many women today are no different than me at that time.

In my journey to forgive this particular ex, I have not felt towards him as I did with the other men I married. God supernaturally gave me the ability to completely release him after many years of trying to salvage what we had left. As a man, I saw his true heart and the potential of who God had created him to be. Sadly, a person cannot want deliverance more than the one needing it. His heart was hardened and he willfully chose to do what he had did, but it sent me into a pivotal point of finding my identity in Christ.

A Turning Point

After he left me the last time when we were living together, it was a very devastating period for me. When I reached out to my family, they wanted nothing to do with the whole mess again. For the first time in my life, I was renting a room in my 50s. It was not something I thought I would ever do.

God was faithful and He opened the door for me to live with one of the staff pastors and her family at the local church I was attending at that time. The couple were in their 30s, with young children, and a beautiful Husky dog. At first, it was so hard to believe where I was at in my life. I was numb, isolated, and broken. Yet, I was undone by all of the support this family gave me.

I learned to adapt to my surroundings and was finally on my road to recovery. They became my adopted family in having a son and daughter, along with grandbabies, and even a grand doggy. Although life was not perfect, I was home for a season with them and grateful to finally be able to *just take care of myself.*

As I recovered, this family blessed me beyond words. For instance, my ex had me give up my vehicle, so he could purchase one that we were supposed to use together. Obviously, when he left the marriage, I was left with no car, and it traumatized me so much. I was paying for Lyft to drive me everywhere and that was a car payment in itself. Once again, I had lost everyone and various things that had mattered to me. I remained with a few items from my mother, some things I had kept when I had my own home, and my clothing.

My adopted family blessed me with everything I needed to heal, including giving me a car for FREE that they had. Although I chose to pay rent, they never asked me for a dime on anything. I was definitely being taught about compassion, unconditional love, and what God's provision for me looked like by living with my adopted family. It took me a while to accept being loved by others, because I did not know what that meant. What I had been through was never God's will for me, but He used it all in the end.

As my healing process continued, I did much soul searching, praying, crying, and wanting to die over and over again. My adopted family accepted me, (flaws and all), gave me the space I needed to be me, along with the security I needed to heal. We became the family I never had and I saw God's hand of mercy and grace tremendously.

This time in my life led me to find out what I was made of and what unconditional love is all about. My adopted family did not have to take me in, *but they did.* I will forever be grateful to God and them who I refer to as, *"My Sweeties."* In the midst of a very challenging time for me, I began to see my purpose in life did not need to revolve around *a man.* For me, that was HUGE!

5

Alone and Married

❖   ❖   ❖

IT WAS A RAINY AFTERNOON AND I WAS IN MY ROOM FEELING DEPRESSED and alone, even though I was married. My mate sat in the living room for hours channel surfacing, as he had done so many times before. As I processed where my life was in this particular marriage, it hit me – I was *alone* and married – I was not in a marriage. I was living as a roommate with my spouse.

That night, I went to bed in such a discouraged state of mind that I did not want to wake up the next morning. I was a Christian, but I was a miserable one. To avoid being home that afternoon when my mate got there, I did what I had always done. I packed up a bag and went to my mothers, as it was the only place where I felt safe and at home. If my mate wanted to treat me as if I was not there, then I would not be. I had grown so tired of that type of disrespect.

In all my years of caring for my mother, she endured the tragedy of seeing me go through one broken relationship to another and it was heart wrenching for her. As we grew closer in our years together, I understood her more in what she had endured being married to my father. In various areas of my life, I was walking in the same shoes she had been in. I began to understand why I related to her pain all too well.

As a child, I remember her usually being alone and my father always working. When they were together, all they did was fight and the beatings she endured by him were brutal. Sadly, this would become my way of life in being married and alone later. My mother also suffered from Broken Heart Syndrome, (BHS), and that is something that can literally cripple a person to death.

Since children are what they live with, I relived my parent's way of life in each broken marriage I was in. As a very lost person in a world of pain and suffering, I became unable to function. I struggled with my identity, weight, and soul constantly and had very little peace of mind. There were days where I did not know if I was coming or going, which caused me to wonder if I would ever be able to be happy.

In this time of finding out who I was and regaining my voice, I ran a lot from people, places, and things. Isolation became my best friend, as I coped to live one more day. Life became overwhelming and I was okay not engaging much with others or too much in any of my marriages. I lived in a state of being, *"stuck,"* mentally, emotionally, and spiritually. I basically became a recluse.

Many times I would have to purpose staying on a job or around people when all I wanted to do was *run*. I knew I was in trouble when I embraced being married and alone more than being with my mate, family, or friends. I was settling and everything in me was SCREAMING not to.

After my last divorce and for first time in my life, I had no one to care for or feel obligated to stay with. It was just me and God, but I would have to face the reality that I had been abandoned, (more than once), by those I had loved and who claimed to love me. This was gut wrenching, because I have loved them with everything I had in me only to be left later.

Being Left and Alone

I think the hardest thing to do is be in a marriage and feel left and alone. One gets married to have someone to do life with. Companionship is so huge in relationships that when it is taken away, one truly suffers. The other great disappointment I had in all of my marriages were that *I wanted to be married more than they did.*

Something that hurt me greatly was when one of my former mates and I were at odds he would purposely not wear his Wedding Ring.

It was a stab to my heart each time he did this, especially due to his unfaithfulness. The first time I found out about one of his affairs, I sold my first Wedding Ring. I no longer wanted to even carry his name or have anything to do with being known as his wife.

It also affected me negatively when I would see a man without a ring and know that he *was* married. Some couples do not care, because they hold the belief that they know they are married in their hearts. Yet for me, wearing a Wedding Ring says something about the commitment in the vows taken on one's wedding day.

I truly believe in covenant marriage not, *"contract,"* ones, so what is the difference? In a covenant marriage, one is truly loved unconditionally, as God loves us. In a contract marriage, it is all about self-protecting and what is in it for the other person, *"You do this for me and I will do that for you."* There is no safety, trust, or security either and that is not how God loves us. As I have healed more, I now do not allow dysfunctional behaviors or any type of abuse to continue in my relationships.

I also studied what strongholds were and how they kept me bound in not being able to heal. It all stemmed from soul trauma. How could I accept love from others when I had been subjected to being abused, left, rejected, abandoned, and uncared for? I could not. My ability to be able to do so for others stemmed from me giving to them what I so desperately needed and wanted for myself *from them.*

Many of you reading this may be on the same healing journey in trying to find out your identity, purpose, and how to love. Please know that my heart and prayers are with you as you travel through these paths of recovery. I invite all of you to rise up with me and remember who we are, what your worth is, and not ever be defined by another's perceptions, words, or views.

Abused women are a, *"unique breed,"* with some serious battle wounds and scars from the fights we have endured to survive. The challenging thing is that what we have been through was something we never asked for. Those who live in abuse stay hidden, because of the shame of what they live in. They are silenced by their addict/abusers with threats of being more abused. Sadly, abuse victims live in prison within their own homes. I know I did for years and many never knew it either.

Behind Closed Doors

Some of the things I encountered behind closed doors were physical, verbal, spiritual, financial, and emotional abuse, along with being controlled, and manipulated. Due to the shame associated with it or the fear of suffering consequences, this way of living was not something that I wanted anyone to know about either.

This included lots of isolating, shunning, shaming, and the silent treatment regularly from my addict/abusers. They would also, *"go into their caves,"* and could stay there for days, weeks, months, and even years. Yet, in public I was treated differently, so that others would not know I was being abused. Sadly, addict/abusers operate in complete narcissism and hypocrisy regularly.

I remember a Supervisor that one of my former mates worked with say to me that he never heard anything negative from my ex in who I was, as his wife. Actually, he would tell them how much he was in love with me, but his actions where well-hidden and *very* different from how I was treated at home. He was shocked that I thought my ex was having an affair with one of the Branch Managers on the job.

This is why when I would end a marriage with an addict/abuser, I was shunned by others, my family, and even various church members from where I attended at that time. In their eyes, I was the insane one in the relationship. I even had my own family member say to me, *"What did you do to set him off?"*

In all of my marriages, there were the Honeymoon Stages we would go through after there were fall outs between us, but that did not last too long. Eventually, something would get triggered and the vicious cycle of abuse would start all over again. We would be like two ships passing in the night living like roommates under the same roof.

It caused so much trauma and I continually felt like I was waiting for the rug to be pulled out from under me and then there was the physical abuse. One ex pulled chunks of my hair out, leaving me with a bloody nose, black and blue eyes, and bruises all over my body. Yet, the rapes from my second ex-husband were the most horrific and I have blocked them out.

In the midst of it all, I *looked* like I had it all together, along with wearing many masks to keep myself from being asked too many questions. If I did share with others what was going on, they wanted no part of, *"becoming involved."* This only added to me feeling like I was not able to trust anyone, let alone my own ex-husband's family or mine.

It pushed me further away from feeling secure or protected. I began to see everyone as an unsafe person that I could not share the *real me* with. This then set me up for a disoriented way of living and that lasted for quite some time, until I got the right type of help for myself.

Plus, these types of relationships had been my way of life for way too long, which led me to being so embarrassed to share with others that I was in the same vicious cycle *again*. I had enough of that to last me a life time. People just did not understand that someone is programmed through fear to stay in abusive situations. No one wakes up in the morning and chooses to live that way. The imprints of abuse are devastating and many think it is only, *"physical,"* but that is not true. Addict/Abusers suffer from many mental issues and so do their victims.

Intimacy Anorexia, (IA)

In 2020, I began to study on what this term meant, which is someone who, *"love starves,"* others out of their woundedness. I then began to study Dr. Douglas Weiss' materials on sexual addictions. He is an Author, Speaker, Licensed Psychologist, and Marriage Counselor, who specializes in sexual addictions. He is also the Founder and President of the American Association for Sex Addiction Therapy, (AASAT), as well as the Clinical Director of Heart to Heart Counseling Center in Colorado Springs.

Dr. Weiss was the first person who began talking about IA that I had ever heard of and is the leading expert on the topic. Hearing what he shared revolutionized my world and gave me the answers to the many questions that had plagued me. As I furthered my education with his materials, it made so much sense that my healing became more targeted in these particular areas of sexual addiction. It was a whole new world opening up to me that I had no clue even existed.

I saw that not only did I choose mates that were IAs, but I *became* one out of the fear in being rejected, raped, or abandoned in my marriages. It was my way of self-protecting and it was very unhealthy. The mindsets of an IA entail many different dynamics which were:

1. Overworking or keeping oneself busy, so they do not connect with their spouses or partners.
2. Blaming others for the problems in their relationships.
3. Limiting or withholding love from someone, especially in the way that a person would want to receive it.
4. Purposely not engaging in giving praise or sex.
5. Being spiritually limited or not participating in things with someone, (i.e., refusing to go to church or pray with them).
6. Unwilling or incapable of share feelings with others, especially in romantic relationships.
7. To control others, using anger or silence against them.
8. Ongoing or unwarranted criticism of those closest to them, but not to others.
9. Monitoring or shaming someone around money issues, especially their mates.

An IA benefits from being *distant*. Marriage is the only relationship where God requires a couple to be spiritually, emotionally, and physically intimate. While everyone else thinks the IA is wonderful, the ones living with them are severely abused and neglected.

Throughout my years of being in these types of relationships, I began to have weight issues and I was usually confused or had, *"brain fog,"* along with many other ailments. Sadly, my mates, (who were all IAs), would then shame me by saying, *"There is something wrong with you,"* and never owned that there abusive treatment of me contributed to the problems in the marriage or what I was experiencing.

After going through my own process of healing from being an IA and why, it was then that I began to see a change in me. It lead me to begin focusing a majority of my coaching on that particular subject, along with Partner Betrayal Trauma, (PBT). I also learned about the spiritual entities that come in through these types of behaviors. With every psychological issue I faced, (or soul wound I had), there was an open door to being tormented in the Spiritual Realm.

Being an IA comes with many other dynamics and it takes a lot of hard work to get to the other side of it, but it can be done. IAs are okay with living like roommates, while their mate is dying to be loved and it has taken me years to finally understand it in myself. Was it easy to do? No, but I am continuing to invite God into this areas daily.

Is There Hope?

Of course there is, but the key is for an individual to become knowledgeable on the issues they may have within themselves *first* and then to own their part in why their relationships have suffered. There must be transparency, honesty, a willingness to change, and a commitment to stick with one's recovery process.

Before addressing any problems within my marriages, my exs and I needed to get personal psychological and spiritual help. Once we worked on our own healings first, then the work could begin to heal the marriages. Sadly, each one of them chose not to do the work and went off in their addictions or with the other women. However, they always would come back later wanting to reconcile or have some form of relationship with me. As the saying goes, *"The grass is not always greener on the other side. You still have to mow it to."*

For the sake of trying to salvage my marriages, I did the work to change with the hopes of reconciliation. Yet, the impact of living in this type of trauma presented many problems for me to heal, as I wanted the relationships to be restored more than they did. The other dilemma I faced was that I felt that I truly missed God in choosing the wrong mates out of my brokenness.

This only led me to press into God more to see things from His perspective. It was not my intent to live the way I was. I just needed help. Despite my mates not being on the same page in trying to salvage our marriages, I learned to seek, *"The why behind the what,"* in my decision making and life choices.

With God, all things are possible, and it is what I have founded what I do and believe in. He never wastes a hurt I go through and I am still evolving into all He has called me to be. Without the proper tools to navigate our life courses, we will hit some bumps in the roads. This is the main reason I wrote this book, so that you can learn from the mistakes I have made.

6

Imprints of Living In Abuse

❖ ❖ ❖

IT WAS A SATURDAY AFTERNOON AND I AWOKE TO THE FEELING OF hopelessness again. I laid in bed curled up, hugging my pillow, and moaning in pain from the top of my head to the soles of my feet. I was alone. I was afraid. I was suicidal. I forced myself to get out of bed. I began to try and *make* myself be happy, but with no success. I took a drive to clear my head.

That did not help, because I got lost on where I was and had more stress trying to figure out how to get home. I felt like my mother did when my parents fought and she and I would take these long drives together. The only difference was that on this day, I was now divorced *again.*

Another birthday had come and gone, which only made me feel more discouraged. I did not understand why my life had to be full of so much abuse. My soul toiled with thoughts of driving off a cliff and dying instantly, but God would not let me take my life no matter how many times I would want to. As I continued to drive aimlessly, I had no clue how I got home. All I knew is that I wanted to desperately stop living in a cycle of chaos and confusion.

As I have taken inventory of my life from before, I had no clue what my worth was and had lost any sense of value for myself. The effects of being raised in abuse, along with what it did to me and our family took a huge part of my life and living as I was had become my, *"normal."*

I was enmeshed with others in such a toxic way that I did not know where I began and other's ended. Family, co-workers, and people's control and opinions of me would end up causing misguided perceptions within myself. Then there was the distortion that love equated, *"sex,"* being planted in me at an early age.

I vaguely remember the molestation between 3 and 4-years of age by a family member. As a child, it sent a very loud, (and wrong), message to me. I learned to find my self-worth in how I looked, not for *who* I was. My value became in my appearance, because it was the only way I would receive recognition.

I was never satisfied with my looks either and tried various diets to lose weight with no long-term success. Food was an issue that I would contend with for a while and still do. I went up and down in my sizes from the age of 12 into my adult years. Later, the pieces started to fall into place as to 'why' weight was an issue for me.

Food and Compulsive Behaviors

It all started one summer when my sister and I went to visit our father, who he had moved to San Francisco for work-related purposes. Our brother was already living there with him, because our mother felt that he was getting into trouble living with her. This was something that damaged my brother deeply, along with other things that had happened between them. He never fully got over things either.

During our time there, we hardly ever saw our father, as he worked all the time. I remember lots of cooking and eating going on and not much time with our Dad. This caused a lot of emotional scaring, especially with our parents no longer being married. He had left her for the woman he was now married to and she was part of our extended family, which made things worse. I became full of resentment and bitterness, but how does at child express that to a father who is emotionally and physically not there? Since I was not able to, an inward cycle of rage continued to spin its ugly wheels inside of me.

While there, my anger continued to grow and I learned to use food as my comfort. I would eat when I was sad, mad, happy, fearful, or depressed, which was a lot of the time. I returned home 20-pounds heavier than when I left that summer and had an issue with food from that point on. This led to my mother making remarks about how I needed to, *"lose weight."* Unknowingly, she left an imprint that I was unacceptable just as I was.

The seed of rejection was already there within me and it began to take a deeper root. Being a compulsive overeater became a full-time job and one of my coping mechanism in managing my pain. It also helped me keep men away or so I thought. Whether I was a size 10 or 18, some men did not care.

I remember one afternoon watching TV and a program came on about obese women. I could relate to much of their pain and how they were stuck in their food addictions, along with being severely depressed. They also shared that there was a Pornographic Community for men who lusted after obese women. One of the women interviewed made her living as an Obese Porn Star and did not want to give up her livelihood, despite her health being at risk. This left me awestruck at how much food controlled people, but that did not stop me in my relationship with it either.

Food had already become my idol, as it was always there for me, never talked back, and did not ask for anything in return. Eating compulsively was not my only problem either. As time went on, shopping became another one of my secret companions. I had accumulated so much debt that when I was laid off from my job of 8-years, I ended up filing for bankruptcy only to get right back into debt over and over again.

Each time a marriage would end, I would struggle just to have enough. Every divorce caused me to become more stressed. Compulsive shopping only contributed to me believing the lie that I was okay, because I had, *"things."* I would seem fine and doing well, but no one knew what was really going on behind the scenes.

Obsessive Compulsive Disorder, (OCD), was my next companion where I would excessively keep things orderly, clean, and never out of place. I learned to structure my life around OCD and would have to allot myself 20 to 30 minutes more to start my day, as I felt I could not leave the house dirty. With OCD, I needed to leave *everything* in order, as it gave me a sense of control over my uncontrollable life.

Another reason I was like this was that in our home growing up, we could not go anywhere on Saturday, unless the *whole* house was cleaned. My sister and I did it resentfully internalizing our anger that our brother did not have to clean. There were definitely two sets of rules we lived by – girls cook, clean, and look pretty, while boys do not belong in the kitchen, are manly, and bring home the bacon.

However, I used my OCD successfully in my professional career and my employers loved me for it. I was the, *"Post It Queen,"* of my office and a perfectionist in my work. This brought me much recognition, but with it also came jealousy from others. Working was an outlet for me and I did not know how to separate it from my home life. I carried my perfectionism in the office into my personal life. Ultimately, it left me stressed most of the time and robbed me of the ability to relax.

This contributed to the other health issues I fought and chronic depression was one of them. Many nights I would lie in bed awake, because I was thinking of all the projects I felt I needed to complete. It also contributed to my weight issues even more, as I would eat late at night with my long work hours. I was tired half of the time and I did not watch what I ate and how many times I would eat. Due to me being a compulsive eater, this fed into my eating addiction even more.

Then there were the catered company events, having the company credit card that gave me money to spend on bringing in staff meals, and all the leftovers that I would be so willing to take home. The added pounds to my 5 $^{2"}$ body frame only caused more pressure to my heart. As I continued to gain weight, the issues with high blood pressure and cholesterol also set in, along with a chemical imbalance.

My weight issues caused me to avoid taking pictures or even having much of a social life. I felt I was fat, did not fit into my cloths, and I was just too exhausted to do anything. My life became a routine of going to work, coming home, and trying to sleep, only to have to wake up early the next morning to do it all over again. This vicious cycle would catch up to me later.

No Sense of Worth

Others perceptions left an imprint on my core being, especially the people I chose to allow into my inner circle and heart. I traced it back to where my sense of worth began to diminish and it all started with feeling rejected by my father. There was also the *conditional* love from friends, past employers, co-workers, and unhealthy relationships that were in and out of my life with men adding more to seeing myself as, *"damaged goods."*

Their imprints of abandonment were all over me, with the message by how I was treated that, *"You are not wanted, important, valued, or loved."* I was looking to fill the void within me that the fatherless little girl had. The worth I held in my father's eyes, (along with the men I had chosen), was not much. I was a woman who had believed the lies of others and I knew no other way to think. I found my sense of worth in how much they loved or did not love me, sadly.

To trust was unthinkable for me and getting help was definitely not something I took lightly. Throughout my life, I grew tired of the lack of progress in my healing. I had tried various 12-Step Programs, only to feel like I just did not fit in. When I would attend them, it would end up with me helping others who were struggling. I left those meetings feeling like the help I needed was not there for me. In the midst of my own pain, I was a Life Coach at heart even back then. I truly was loved by God, but I could not see it.

However, I had been given the ability to take nothing and turn it into something, which flowed through me so easily. I was blessed with writing, working in Administration, and helping others feel encouraged and hopeful about themselves. Yet, I could not see any of those qualities, despite my work and appearance reflecting a strong and confident woman.

I became two people in one, losing myself in each of them. I was not the person I thought I should be and the real person behind closed doors was depressed, anxious, compulsive, and very angry. I did not know how to allow myself the pleasure of being, *"free,"* because it was a foreign word to me.

I had to learn how much God really did love me that He would send Jesus to die for me and mankind. I had been told I was worthless so many times that I had learned to believe it.

My Sexual Identity

In this area of my life, I lost my innocence and my identity way before I even knew what it all meant. It confused me, causing me to become ashamed about pretty much anything that pertained to sexual intimacy. I felt dirty, used, and I viewed the actual act as something unenjoyable. The way I was introduced to my sexual identity was not at all how God intended it to be.

My years in school were very challenging also, as I physically blossomed early in my teens. I was called one particular celebrity's name, who was known for her large bust line. Due to this, some boys only gave me attention to see how far they could go with me. They did not see me as someone who had feelings and were very cruel to me. This only added to becoming more confused about me identity, as a woman.

I remember this one particular time when I had decided to go with friends to a party and there was drinking and drugs being used. I felt like an outcast amongst my friends, so I decided to drink in order to be accepted and became very intoxicated. I was also being closely watch by the boys there.

There was a parked Van outside of the home of where this party was being held at. A boy asked me to go in it with him. I was flattered and did so only to be exposed to him trying to force me to have sex with him. When I did not give in, he left the Van, and spread rumors that I led him on calling me a, *"Big Tease."* I was crushed and later that would become what other boys would know me by. I was the talk of the evening and could not even remember what fully took place the next day.

Eventually, I decided not to focus on boys at all, but to put my efforts into my schooling. However, I could not see my full potential and I was still trying to win the approval of others. What I saw and felt was being ugly, fat, not popular, and that I did not fit in anywhere. As an adult, this fell over into becoming involved with unsafe and unhealthy men.

I had become involved in relationships for all the wrong reasons. I was longing to be loved and due to being subjected to sexual abuse, I equated being loved with having sex. With each one of my exs, I engaged in pre-marital sex, sadly. I then would feel such condemnation and an obligation to marry them. It is how I was programmed to believe through my family, who operated in a religious spirit. I literally married ever man I slept with.

The programing I had carried itself into all of my marriages, causing me to become incapable of enjoying any form of sexual encounters. Being objectified at a young age will do that to a person and I performed sexually, because that is all I knew to do. As time went on, I began to see how unfulfilled I was in all of my marriages, until the day came where I stopped performing, (and feeling), all together. This only caused me to withdraw and become less accommodating to my addict/abuser mates. Ultimately, they all chose to go to other women, instead of staying with a good one and working it through.

It has been a literal miracle that this area of my life has been redeemed and that I am able to understand how God created me sexually. Unfortunately, I would face many more years of abuse and trauma before I would understand who I was created to be, as a woman.

My Pain

The more pain I would experience, the more I became resentful, bitter, and full of irritation. I felt betrayed by those that I would try to be perfect for. I would scream inside of my head, *"I never asked to be born into all of this mess!"* To keep the peace, I would then do my best to try and rescue or fix them. Self-protection reigned deep within me and I would not show any type of fear or cry. All the unresolved issues I was carrying towards others led me to stuffing my emotions even further down.

"You should have..." were the words I heard most of my life and this only fed into my perfectionistic way of thinking. I was doing and saying all the right things to be loved, but to no avail was it reciprocated. There was also the spiritual side of me that was so distorted in how I saw God. The lies of the enemy were literally burned into my mind about who I was and how God made me.

The thought, *"There must be something wrong with me that I am not loved or wanted,"* and the enemy wanted to keep me in that mindset. Then to add fuel to the fire of my pain, I had also been exposed to the occult in my teen years, as I shared about in Chapter 3.

After having my only child and being separated from my first husband, the man that had first abused me came back into my life again. He showed up unannounced at my home and I could see that he had been using some form of drug, which later turned out to be Cocaine. We began to argue and he became possessed with rage. He actually grab my child from me claiming he was going to take her away, if I did not do what he wanted. I could see the demonic over him and somehow I managed to get him out of my home, but do not know how.

All I remember after he left was trying to calm my baby down. She was traumatized from what had just taken place and was screaming from the top of her lungs. I felt as if I was losing my mind and I finally got her to fall asleep. I went into the bathroom, looked into the mirror, and broke into tears.

I was so distraught that suicidal thoughts came into my mind to cut my wrists and bleed to death. The demonic was whispering in my soul strongly as I battled within. Being subjected to what I had just experienced will do that to a person, as it was abuse and trauma not only to myself, but to my baby.

Then I looked over at my child and thought about how it would affect her to grow up knowing that her mother killed herself. I just could not do that to her. I truly believe that if it was not for my child, I would not be here today. I was dealing with severe stress mixed in with post-pardon depression, causing me to become even more fearful of what the future would hold for me and my newborn baby.

The next time I would be plagued with suicidal thoughts was when I was in my second marriage. I was so miserable, distraught, and overwhelmed with my life that I almost took a whole bottle of anti-depressants that had been prescribed to me. I would often think of how I could kill myself by driving off a cliff, doing a family suicide, or run into oncoming traffic hoping to die instantly. With so much pain plaguing me, thoughts of going home to heaven where continual, but fear stopped me that I would live in eternal damnation, if I killed myself.

Unfortunately, life continued to only get worse. I still had not come to terms with my past and how I buried my pain deep within me. The illnesses that I was experiencing began to weigh on my body, but I put them aside focusing on everything and everyone else. I bypassed taking care of myself, which led to many years of misery and more pain. I would later be diagnosed with other ailments in the midst of learning that my third husband was having an affair. All of this caused my body to shut down and my doctor ended up taking me out of the work force for a year to heal.

It was then that I was faced with the reality of my life – I struggled with who I was, where I was going, and what was my identity as a woman, wife, and mother. I could not believe what was happening with to me, which pushed me more into denial that I went numb inside. There was such a stronghold on my mind, will, and emotions that it ended up causing me to almost have a nervous breakdown.

A Lesson Learned

The abuse in my life came in so many forms, but so did God's love to sustain me. As I continually purposed to surrender it all, there were such tender moments in my deepest hours of need. Although I kept stumbling back into the same dysfunctional pattern in my relationships, God was merciful to me. I never felt condemned by Him and had a sense of unconditional love in my times of great sorrow. He was, (and still is), very patient with me.

As hard as it was to go through living in abuse, I knew Jesus understood me. He endured the worst abuse of all to give me my salvation and a future in eternity. I could embrace that He knew my pain all too well and find the assurance of His compassion in the midst of what I was going through.

As the years progressed, I became more aware of the demonic realm and how there were, "cycles," of abuse past down from generation-to-generation in my family lineage. It was then that God began to show me about spiritual warfare and how to battle the enemy with what I had been exposed to in the occult. It took a while to learn how to rise up and use it against the demonic realm later. I then began to become a militant Spiritual Warrior that the demonic could no longer reckon with.

I could see that much of the pain I went through were by demonic programming, lies, and the soul wounds inflicted on me by others. The pattern of dysfunction is how satan likes to keep a person in bondage. I had suppressed much of the traumas, but that would not last. My dreams and body were all speaking to me on what I had forgotten.

Ultimately, the pain I went through was not in vain and God began to show me how to use it to my advantage. I could stay a, *"victim,"* or become a, *"victor."* Being a victim was easy to do, because it required me to stay stuck. Being a victor was already won through the Cross and all that Jesus had already done for me.

It was then that I began to take my power back and fight the demons that had plagued me to for far too long. The journey was not, (and still is not), easy, but I have nothing left to lose. I chose not to stay insane, so I could become all He wanted me to be. To do that, I would first have to find out who I was in Him.

7

Programmed Lies

It was another session with a Lay Counselor from our local church. I had been through several of them with some of my exs and I was usually the one made out to be the problem. When I did not stand for it and would call out my exs on the lies they were telling, I was the, *"non-submissive one."* I remember how I would leave each session never wanting to come back.

Then the programming would kick in that I needed to submit to my husband and the process of reconcilation. The problem was that normal counseling *does not work* when one is married to an addict/abuser. I also kept thinking about my mother and how she would stay with my father, despite his abuse of her and his children. I now realize that I only did what I was programmed to do and not of God at all.

Without even knowing it, I taught myself how to self-protect, as there was no safety in my family. I thought that it was something I would learn to live with. As I began to heal, I could see the different types of mindsets that were unconsciously built into me. Abuse taught me to always be in a, *"fight or flight,"* mode.

A life of safety and security was foreign to me, let alone a reality. It taught me to never let my guard down and live on the edge of being suspicious most of the time. When I was caught off guard and began to remotely trust, being abused was right around the corner. I learned to always have a Plan B when Plan A did not work.

I wanted to feel safe, loved, secure, and at peace within my heart and soul. Sadly, it was ingrained in me that those things were just, *"fantasy thinking."* I became a woman who was ruled by seven major areas of programmed lies, which then led me to pick relationships that would keep me in those lies. I share about them later on in the book.

I also learned the power of mind control and how it is used all over the world today. People think it is not real, but it is used in the most elite Governmental Programs today. Some of our top officials know about this and are themselves programmed by demonic entities that they have surrendered their lives to in order to have power, prestige, and wealth.

For those who stay faithful to the programmed lies they have believed by the enemy, they are in for a rude awakening later when their time comes to cross over. The pleasure in sin they had for the temporal riches of this earth will soon fade away. There is always one thing cults have in common – self. It is all about worldly pleasures, self-centeredness, and selfishness.

Satan distorts everything that God says and I have learned to believe that, *"Truth taken to the extreme is error."* When living for God becomes a bunch of rules and regulation with shame and guilt attached to it, there is something wrong. I loved God, so I did what I was told, but always knew that there had to be more to living for Christ. It was satan's plan to truly destroy my destiny and identity, but God would not let him.

What I Was Taught About Myself

Spiritually | My Identity in Christ: I remember when I first learned about God's love towards me. It did not resemble what I was taught about His conditions to be accepted. Being abused also taught me to believe that I was unlovable, because of the way I looked. What I was exposed to by cult members through my SRA abuse imbedded pure fear within me about God.

The message given to me when my father left our family was there was something wrong with me. I later took that lie into my adulthood thinking that who I was did not measure up to who I thought I should be. It alienated me from others, especially those in my family. It also made me an angry person and I became bold, confrontive, and outspoken, which also did not go over well with the men in my family.

I found myself with the inability to connect with the males in my family, especially my father. This in turn hindered my relationship with Father God. Being raise as I was, there were many religious traditions about who God. It led me to believe that He would be mad at me, if I was not, *"perfect."* I could relate to Jesus and the Holy Spirit, but Father God was the one I stayed cleared from.

The fathers I saw in my family were very strong and independent men, who did not have time to be religious. They were self-made, and believed that it was them that made things happen. It was not until later in my life that I learned to accept being fully known, loved, and freely forgiven by, *"Papa God,"* as I refer to Him now.

Personally – Who I Thought I Was: There were four thoughts about myself that stood out to me continually: 1) hopeless; 2) damaged goods; 3) not enough; and 4) unworthy. In the deepest part of my soul I wanted to believe that I was not these things, but I had a very hard time doing so. I believed that I was incapable of being loved by anyone for too long, because of my past. This was only confirmed with every abusive relationship I entered into ending in being rejected and abandoned, despite their being vows taken before God to stay married, *"until death do us part."*

I truly felt that, if the work had been done to mature, heal, and get the right tools implemented, my marriages could have been salvageable. Yet, every relationship would tragically end leaving me with more brokenness inside. It altered my view on who I thought I was created to be as a person, woman, wife, mother, and woman of God. The continual rejections and disappointments seared a mark of deep trauma within my soul.

I remember the times when I would look in the mirror and be repelled by my own reflection. I was never taught my worth and appearance was everything, which made it easy for me to be objectified. The hard work of unraveling the lies of who I thought I was has finally help me change into a totally different person.

Relationships

<u>Relationally | The People in My Life</u>: Trying to earn people's friendships and love was what turned me into a people-pleaser. I do not remember having any form of relationship where there were, *"no strings attached."* When men saw that I was so easily accommodating to meet their needs just to feel loved, I was used and left high and dry later. It is a tool that satan uses to break women down, as he has a disdain for us in who we are. After all, it was through a woman that Jesus was born.

Since I did not know how to have healthy relationships, I settled for whatever someone would give me. Then when I married, I tried to be what I was *expected* to be in the bedroom, but there was never any true intimacy. Since I was violated at such a young age, I had no clue what a healthy lovemaking was between couples.

I never felt good about being intimate and it was not that I was the only one with the problem. My mate's sexual mindsets were all birthed out of their own sexual addictions and not on what God calls love making to be. Such distortion only took me further down the road to feeling lost in my relationships with the men in my world. It has been a long road to my recovery in learning what, *"True Love,"* is really all about, but I am grateful to be on the right track. The people I use to allow in my life are no longer around either. I have learned to choose more wisely who comes into my inner circle and it has helped my healing process tremendously.

<u>Rationally | How I Thought</u>: This has been an area of contention for me and there are times where I had to stop my thought process all together. It was the only way to keep my sanity. There were various demonically induced programs and trigger words that would take over my soul at times. Things escalated to levels in my cognitive thinking that caused me to live in much soul trauma, if I was not careful to manage how my mind worked. The demonic forces that plagued me would want me to see, (and believe), things that were simply not true. My awareness to the demonic was heightened. I would see demons at night standing in my bedroom doorway haunting me, along with noises and voices that no one else could hear. I would have dreams of me descending to a bottomless pit that was full of fire to fight the demonic forces that came my way.

The interesting thing was that I was not afraid of them, but was empowered by the Spirit of God to be fierce and untouchable. I would always win every battle that came my way and fear had no grip on me in those types of dreams. I was confident, secure, and a victor every time. It was like I was a Vatican Warrior that was equipped to fight with a tenacity I had never known before.

In my waking life though, it was a different story. I was the total opposite of who I saw in my dreams. I later learned about Dissociative Identity Disorder, (DID). This is where two or more identities, (or personalities), alternate in controlling my consciousness and behaviors. In being ritualistically abused, I would suppress what took place to survive emotionally. DID is when my personalities, *"split,"* so I could survive the torment.

I learned how to break free from all of this through having Inner Healing and Spiritual Deliverance Sessions with trained individuals that God led me to. I also studied about the programming that is done through the demonic realm by individuals who are trained to do this in satanism and occults. Sadly, these individuals are in high-ranking positions and use the air waves to do so, also known as, *"energy forces."* It is also all part of the New Age Movement.

As I pursued my deliverance, a Warrior for Christ was birthed in me. The devices that the enemy tried to destroy me with where later developed by God into being my Weapons of Warfare. I become the, *"voice for the voiceless,"* who could not fight on their own. To overcome, I reprogrammed my mind with the Word of God, therapy, and my educational training in various areas. I began to experience breakthroughs and peace started to fill my life more.

How to Feel

<u>Emotionally | My Soul, (the Mind, Will, and Emotions)</u>: My emotional make-up was definitely skewed and it changed how I perceived everything around my world. As I grew in my faith and learned about the deliverance of the soul, I recognized that the, *"fear of man,"* ruled me much. I was too emotionally unbalanced to see myself. I usually felt like

people had ulterior motives towards me, especially men. In this area, nine times out of ten, I was correct that their motives were not pure and I paid dearly for it later. Satan knew my weak spot of looking for love to fill the void that only God could and he used it very well against me.

This caused me to not have my will in alignment with what God wanted for me, which fed my toxic emotions. The interesting thing is that many women I knew would have the same mindsets about themselves. It just proved that satan does play on our emotions and he uses the same lies on everyone.

With women, I would see a patterns of much contention, competition, jealousy, gossip, and backbiting. As I observed why this was happening, I understood that the soul wounds of rejection comes in many forms. When their souls are ruling them, women are mainly the ones that tend to have their hormones unbalanced. While the men in my family dealt with their pain through work or addictions, the women had to learn to manage their emotions or be labeled as being out of balanced.

God began to give me discernment in understanding people's hearts and I learned to see who was safe and who the, *"wolves in sheep's clothing"* were. My emotions started too stabilize and I became more knowledgeable on how to test the spirits that were before me in my relationships.

Choices and Behaviors

Volitionally | Free Will to Choose: Despite having a check in my spirit on various things and people, my sense of direction was way off, which lead me to make some very unwise life choices. There were times where it was out of ignorance and there were other times when I willfully chose to go against what I sensed was right to do.

I so wanted to be loved, fit in, and appreciated that I would lose all rational. In the end, I would be burnt out, used, and abused, which only took me down some pretty dark roads. When I *willfully* chose to go against God and His Word, it stemmed from the spirit of witchcraft and it is rebellion. It is what satan did when he was kicked out of heaven, (see Isaiah 14 and Ezekiel 28). This then gave him legal access to rule over me and he was able to use sickness against me.

Once I began to choose God's will over mine, I began to submit to Him more and fight spiritually against the enemy. Today, it has made me very in tune to the Spiritual Realm in sensing the presence of evil or of God. This helps me to make choices that are led by discernment and not by compulsive behaviors.

Behaviorally | Formed Patterns: The way I did things based on my past programming caused various patterns to form, which led to much distress. It was a way in which the enemy set me up for failure to cause a delay in what God was calling me to. It then kept me in abusive relationships, mindsets, and behaviors that were toxic.

Those who do not believe in the demonic will think these things are a figment of a person's imagination, but they are wrong. Satan is alive and strong in the minds of many today. For me, the moment I would get out of God's grace and covering, I am immediately given a check within. I would then go back to what I knew is true from His word, my training, and personal growth. This has been my solace in keeping me free from continual pain and trauma.

I also have various Prayer Partners that I am accountable to. The moment I repent, renounce, and divorce myself from what it was that caused me to stray in the first place, I am back on track again. If I have spoken words contrary to what God would want me to, I pray to make all words void that I have spoken and ask for God's forgiveness, which is given immediately.

No one is perfect, nor does anyone ever arrive on this side of heaven. The one true lesson I learned was purposing to be better and staying true to God, myself, and what I know is the right thing to do.

8

Broken Trust

I WAS 10-YEARS OLD LIVING IN CALIFORNIA WHEN THE RITUALS BEGAN by my father's cousin, Edie. The Santeria cult had people everywhere and she was the regional witch assigned to the area in which my mother and siblings moved to after our parents divorced. She had a large property with a couple of back houses on it that I distinctly remember and I would have repeated dreams of it. Several years later, I even went by the house to see it and had various flashbacks on things I had suppressed.

A ritual that I do remember was on a hot summer day and I was taken to one of the backhouses. I saw a children's portable swimming pool on the floor filled with water and flowers floating in it. The room was lite with candles and had incense burning. Even today, I cannot stand the smell of incense and what it represents. Edie sternly told me to take off my cloths, get into the pool, and stand in the middle of it. I was paralyzed with fear and then she yelled, *"Do it now!"*

There was a strong presence of evil, while Edie stood there smoking a cigar, drinking Vodka, and spewing it out of her mouth all over me. It stung my eyes and I cringed in pain keeping them closed while she continued the ritual. I could hear her chanting in demonic tongues, so I took a peek. I was shocked to see her eyes rolled back and she was in a full blown trance. Suddenly, she looked directly at me. They were not *her* own eyes anymore either. They became snake eyes that were blood red and she definitely had become demon possessed. She also hissed like a snake when she spoke all kinds of incantations.

She wore a multi-colored outfit that resembled something from Africa with several beaded necklaces around her neck that represented the demons assigned to her. They were called, *"saints,"* to everyone else though. I do not remember what happened after that, as I must have disassociated. That was the start of experiencing SRA first hand.

I later learned that there had been a curse put on me for destruction should I not become the next witch on the throne from my mother's lineage. This cult used some of the traditions from the Catholic Church, which causes their followers to think that it is okay to do the rituals they do.

One of satan's best tools is using men and women that have, *"a form of godliness,"* to lure people into trusting them, but they are really led by demonic spirits and mind programming. Sadly, there is too much of this in the church where embracing many cult practices are taking place. Why? Because witches and warlocks are assigned to various churches to bring in division and destroy the congregation.

There are even decoy churches and schools that have hidden services and underground SRA going on. The very person who is the Sunday School Teacher or even Pastor are really in disguise and become the evilest cult member at night. Witchcraft is very prevalent in the church in how services are run, traditions are kept, and biblical truths taken out of context used legalistically against people.

As I attended various churches throughout the years, I was one who could see the work of the enemy the moment I would become involved. I struggled with the ability to sense these things, as it was not always good. Some people had such a strong presences of evil that they would manifest against me.

When I would see them in operation and begin to address it within the Leadership, as God led me to, I was ostracized. I ended up withdrawing from various churches, as the spiritual opposition was great, but I did continue to do spiritual warfare for them to be freed. If the church submitted to what God was sharing with them, changes took place, and they grew. If they did not I was led to leave the church, shake the dust off of my feet, and not participate any longer with them.

Other tools the enemy loves to use is gossip and betrayal amongst those who serve the Body of Christ. I have had my share of those two entities more than I would like to remember. I eventually learned how important it is to know the enemy's tactics and to be able to discern well. If I did not, I was the target of attacks later.

Partner Betrayal Trauma, (PBT)

I never knew what this term meant, until I began studying the effects of it through my training. In going through it multiple times and the pain was indescribable. I actually did not start to really heal, until my last divorce. I also saw that betrayal was everywhere in my life and not just in my romantic or married relationships.

I had been betrayed by family, co-workers, people at church, and friends, but nothing compared to learning of the porn, alcohol, or drug addictions from the men in my life. Then there were my exs affairs and some even had children with their mistresses. This was the hardest part, because I could not have children after age 25.

PBT is a complex emotional instability that I did not need to add to my already long list of illnesses. When I realized that I had been betrayed in many of the relationships I was in, it sent my head spinning. I started to understand why I was so smart in certain areas, but so ill equipped in relationships. I researched the mental state I had basically been in all my life and then examined why I could be having them. Ultimately, it all was because of the trauma of betrayal. Here is what I experienced:

1. **PSYCHOLOGICALLY:** I was a hot mess! I experienced triggers that left my stomach in knots. I felt completely damaged with no sense of self-worth on top of my already low self-esteem. Each time I was betrayed by the person that was the closest in the world to me, I thought in some way it was *my fault*. I lost all confidence and felt even more unlovable.

2. **LOSS OF INTEREST**: I would become stuck in my pain and gave up my hobbies, friends, and family. I went into silent

suffering and was clinically depressed and lost my ability to do life.

3. **NIGHTMARES:** PTSD set in through my nightmares about the betrayals, seeing my exs in bed with other women, or in being abandoned.

4. **PREOCCUPIED OR OBESSESED:** I was not able to concentrate on anything except for the betrayals. I could not fathom that my exs could do what they all did to me, especially when they were the people that claimed to love and care for me. I was unable to work and there were days that I was bedridden.

5. **ISOLATION:** I did not want to have to face others and explain things to them about my life. One marriage and divorce to an addict/abuser was bad enough, but *five* was brutal. I lived in isolation from the entire world for days, weeks, and months on end.

A Place to Call Home

Throughout my adult years, I would attend various church gatherings. I was looking for a place to call my, *"Home Church,"* but was not having much success in doing so. Due to my past, not many understood the life of an SRA person, let along someone who had been married so many times.

Then I realized that satan had his talons in every church. If he could not get in by churches being cult driven, he would get in through gossiping, backbiting, or a religious spirit. Sometimes the jezebel spirit was over various individuals, which caused me to stay clear of some women's gatherings and even attending church in person for a while.

With the life experiences I had under my belt, I did not allow just anyone into my personal life. In my faith walk, God has lovingly led me into deeper encounters with Him through seasoned Believers, who I have grown to respect.

These individuals operate in the prophetic, pray in the Spirit, believe that miracles still happen today, and that all the gifts of the Spirit are alive and well. God used them to help me renew my mind and deprogram the lies of the enemy through prayer and an intimate relationship with Himself. As I matured, what were road blocks to my getting better became stepping stones to heal.

When I finally was able to align myself in the identity and love of Christ, developing my spiritual life and character became my normal. I did not want to partner with carnality anymore. I stopped blaming others, began taking responsibility for things, and stopped expecting everyone else to pave the way for me.

I had to balance my thought life in God and not by what I saw or heard around me. There was just too many mixed ideologies on God, faith, family, and it only made me lukewarm in the end. I became more confused and stressed out trying to conform to what I saw others doing. I had to learn what it was that God wanted *me* to be doing.

Understanding what the Bride of Christ was all about caused me to rise up and take my rightful place by Jesus. That meant facing the pain of my past with God and watching for confirmations the Holy Spirit would give me on who was safe to allow in my life and who was not. I literally had to stay away from men for a while, which enabled me to finally begin becoming whole again.

Safety at All Costs

Like anyone else, I wanted to have friends, a fun life, make memories, and be part of a group where I was accepted. After each divorce, I would have to find another church to attend, because my reputation was completely ruined by my exs.

I often felt like an outcast in being subjected to SRA and in going through more than one divorce. What others found interesting, I did not. What some ministries put their efforts into advancing the Kingdom of God was not what I was called to do. I was okay with no longer leading, but on the front lines in the Spiritual Realm contending for whatever church God would lead me to.

I purposed not to be entangled in any church gossip and there were people that I would have to exit in having relationships with. I was once the topic of others conversations, (and not in a good way either), so not being around any form of backbiting was a boundary I would laid for myself.

As I dealt with a variety of triggers and emotions, God would led me to specific people for help. Living in isolation was not going to help me see the light at the end of the tunnel anymore either.

I committed myself to seeing a Christian therapist once a week. I also had my spiritual family that were very instrumental in caring for me in my greatest time of need. My spiritual daughter would have such a listening ear when I was going through things. I can see her beautiful big eye before me right now, as I write this.

Being secure was a huge thing for me and I did not realize how fragile I was, until I finally accepted the reality of my world. Living with my new family taught me somethings. I learned about what a parent-child relationship should and should not look like by how they were with their own children.

In my relationship with them, they were kind, patient, let me be me, and never asked for anything other than to heal. As I continued to live with them, the wounded little girl inside of me grew and began to find out what I had missed in my own family growing up. My life began to have some form of stability and I was able to stay peaceful more than feeling like a burden to others.

Staying True To What I Know

As I have aged, I realize that I am different in many ways than other women. What I have found to be of interest before is not anymore. My personal convictions have changed in how I speak, dress, and communicate with others. I am seeing the errors of my ways and choose to stop trying to, *"be right,"* all the time. I know enough from scripture that when there is strife going on, there is every other evil work. The book of James clearly talks about in Chapter 3.

I knew it was wise to only have men in my life that were married to women I knew or coached. As I would observe even those marital relationships, I found myself being grateful that God had delivered me from my past. In many relationships, I saw such unhappiness, division, and tension, along with the undercurrent of bitterness and unforgiveness brewing.

As time went on, I was able to know what I wanted and to accept that I did not need to have a man on my arm to feel validated. I could stay true to what I knew was right for me. Yet, it was hard to accept the truth of my Life Story when I realized that I had been legally married from the ages of 19 to 58, but never in a *real marriage*.

I saw that marriage God's way did not remotely resemble what I came out of. Many today still believe that staying in abusive relationships is God's will. It is *not*. It only keeps a person entangled in double-mindedness and abuse longer than they need to be. God met me right there in the midst of it all. Ultimately, nothing worth fighting for is easy and I finally accepted the fact that, *"I was worth fighting for!"*

When the Corona Virus hit, I was isolated for over two-years and laid off from a position I had in the Healthcare Industry. It was an overall traumatizing experience for the world and I contracted COVID-19 twice. This is where the fight to life came in when I thought I would die. It was also in those years that I found myself.

9

Surviving the Coronavirus Pandemic

In 2020, I never thought that I would be subjected to what I was. Early in March, I contracted the Coronavirus and was double quarantined in my home, along with there being no vaccine available yet. Not only could I not go out in public, I was confined to my bedroom. I literally felt like I was fighting for my life from the demonic torment that plagued me during the night.

I would lie in my bed sweating profusely with a fever of over 100 degrees. My vision was blurry, chest pounding, and every part of my body felt sore. I had been sick before, but never like this and I contracted the three times more than once within a 3-year period, even *after* receiving the vaccinations. Each time I did, I felt like I was in two worlds at one time – heaven and hell. I was delirious from high fevers and I could not even speak or think clearly. In my desperation, I silently cried out to God.

As this pandemic swept across our world like a plague from the Old Testament, life came to a halting stop for so many while others lost their lives. Many businesses lost so much income that many had to close their doors permanently. There was such a panic all over that many did not know what their futures held and I was one of them.

My isolation was none stop to avoid infecting anyone. There came a point where I was happy to die and I so wanted to. I was not even able to go to the hospital, because I did not meet the criteria for them to take me in. Amongst the elderly, there was so many deaths and I could not be seen just anywhere either.

Since I contracted the virus in its early stages and it was not known how to treat it fully. The reality hit me that it was just me and God in getting to the other side of this horrible time in my life. I was scared, alone, and in a state of severe confusion, pain, suffering, and fear.

It was not until the second week of January in 2022 that I was able to step out into the public again. The virus was such a controversial subject amongst many as to whether to get vaccinated or not, wear a mask or not, and were the targets of so many discussions.

I remember going shopping and seeing people literally get into fights, hoarding paper goods, cleaning products, and food. It was definitely a time of great chaos for everyone that would make history and it has.

Exposure to COVID

I later learned that I became infected when I worked in Patient Health Services for a medical organization. The symptoms were flu-like, headaches, brain fog, not able to breathe well, and deep fatigue. Every morning, I could barely walk and felt like I had been hit by Mack Truck over and over again.

Dying became a mental focus on my worst days. I had studied on what heaven was like and I truly believed it is a real place with so much to offer than this world could ever give me. I longed to be there with friends, family, and loved ones who had gone before me already.

The virus was spreading and continued to do so and there were many Conspiracy Theories floating around. The Healthcare Industry was a wreck with staff shortages, no rooms for those who had been infected, and people dying by the thousands. Due to the exposures, hospitals were flooded and convalescent homes were having to be evacuated with the elderly dying daily. It was a time of shear panic and it did not stop there.

Schools were shut down, employees could not go into work, and everything moved to being done online. People's homes turned into their offices and children could not go to school. However, many other business were birthed, while others were closed. The political issues that the Nation faced were even worst. We had so many riots, terrorist attacks, and then there was the war with Russia and the Ukraine.

Vaccination shots were developed and given to so many people, but they *still* did not stop the virus from spreading. People were suffocating from the fear of death, living paranoid, wearing masks, and isolated in their home. Depression was everywhere, obesity sky rocketed, marriages deteriorated, and church on-line became the norm.

Then there was the Presidential Elections and so much more happening around the world that cause more chaos. The virus would not die and many grew tired, weary, and faint hearted. Life as the world knew it would never be the same and everyone was affected by in one way or another.

Hit Hard

When the virus hit me the first time, I was not prepared for what I would experience. I shut down and refused to engage in anything other than my healing. Have you ever felt like your heart was going to come out of chest with extreme pressure? During this time, that was me. I would lay in bed and feel like there was a steel pole piercing through me.

I equated it with the broken heart I carried with what had transpired throughout my life. In the midst of it, I still could feel some of God's presence. Yet, there were blocks of times that I do not remember. I was in and out of consciousness, as I lay there with a temperature that felt like I was on hot burning coals.

I began to see my life flashing before me. My body ached to the point of despair and my mouth was filled with blisters. Had I not forced myself to get up and shower, bed sores would have definitely developed. I literally was at the brink of life and death. Demons would come to me in my dreams fighting to have my soul. They taunted me nightly from the strongholds the enemy had used from the PTSD I was suffering from.

I had always been a Warrior for Christ, but now I laid at the mercy of God, because I could not fight. When I did have strength, I would text a few people to pray for my life and they did. I fought the depression that plagued me in not having anyone there by my side and the isolation was unbearable at times. I continued to ask God to take my life, but every morning I would wake up again. I was tormented from the depth of my soul and my body was racked with so much pain that I became numb to it.

Day after day, I dealt with more internal suffering, along with the torment of demons hackling in my soul claiming that, *"they had me now."* I finally gave up and stopped praying.

Supernatural Breakthrough

I awoke one morning to a Group Text from a prayer group that I was connected to. I also had texts from two old friends that I would stay connected with. I was so sure that I would die that I had my spiritual family keep an eye out just in case I did not come out of my room. I left my *Last Will and Testament* for them should I pass and crawled up in my bed ready, hoping, and praying to die. Life had no meaning for me anymore. All the strength I once had to fight for what was important to me went out the window.

Then something arose within me – I believe it was from the prayers of all those who were interceding on my behalf. I heard, *"You will not die, but surely live."* I saw the power of Jesus flashing before me in a bright and strong wind. I then captured a picture of Him covering me from the top of my head to the souls of my feet.

He said to me, *"You are not going anywhere, My Bride, for I have too much work for you to do."* I began to find strength in my body, spirit, and soul to be able to pray again. I started to stand on the promises that I had been given by the Holy Spirit. I then went to war in the heavenlies against the demonic assignments satan had against me.

I prayed like I had never prayed before and I was heard by Almighty God. I kept hearing various Scriptures and phrases rise up in my spirit. After a time of warfare, I was back to being able to do life again and my future changed completely. I began to actually believe in, *"Whose,"* I was and the price Jesus paid at Calvary for my full and complete redemption from whatever the enemy would try to throw my way.

Daily I was being healed, set-free, and becoming ready for whatever God had for me, but it did not come without paying a price to sustain my victory. It required me to work really hard to be delivered from the old mindsets, hurts, and traumas of the past. Was it easy? No, but I was committed to the process of getting to the other side.

How I Survived

One of the things I learned during this time was that satan loves to kick you when you are down. He made sure that all the odds were set-up against me. If he could get me in agreement with the spirit of death, he had won, and he sure did try.

Due to battling the spirit of suicide after my mother's passing, I lost my purpose as to why I was on this earth in the first place and basically lost my faith. I literally felt like a modern day Job. Scriptures that I had heard about trials and tribulations being turned around for my good kept coming within my soul.

I still struggled with why I would to stay in this world when everything that I loved and held dear was no longer in my life? It took me some time to realize how this mindset was so contrary to God's heart for my destiny. My life here on earth was not about me, but about doing the will of the Father and I had to re-align myself with that. I went through a purging process of all the filth the enemy had programmed me to believe.

At every opportunity, his demonic lies would try to make me believe that I was nothing, which only inflicted more soul trauma. I was so stuck in everything I was facing, until God's Spirit got a hold of me reminding me who I was created to be. I had to start the tough journey of accepting that I would never have the relationships I wanted. Not only was I mourning the death of my mother, I was grieving the loss of everything, as I knew it to be.

I found my identity in them and that is where the layers of deception began to unfold for my healing to come full circle. I needed to learn that I *was not* defined by my relationships and that despite me not having what I had longed for, my purpose in this life was not over. I saturated myself in how God saw me and that is when my life began taking a turn for the better. Where all my relationships restored? No, but little by little, *I was.*

10

Knowing The Truth

It was one of those afternoons where my ex-husband and I were having that, "*difficult conversation,*" with e-mails going back and forth to one another. We had been separate for years now and we were attempting to reconcile one more time. I never wanted a divorce and would have stayed, if he would have done the work with me to heal the marriage and to get help for his addictions. In this particular conversation, I wanted to know about the affairs he had and why.

One afternoon, I caught him off guard by asking him directly if he had affairs when we lived under the same roof together. I had always believed that he only had them when we were separated. To my surprise, he finally confessed that he *was* having them when we were living together. I went numb inside and then silent. For me to go silent was a miracle. I think I was in shock more than anything else. I always have said that, "*When I stop talking is when one should be worried.*" Why? Because that is when I know that it is futile to try and have a conversation and I then exit the relationship completely.

I began to retrace things that I had found odd in our marriage, but could not put my finger on what was happening. After my ex-husband's confession, I was able to put two and two together and things started to make sense. I was not crazy when I had a gut feeling that he was doing something deceitful. Knowing this truth caused my heart to fall into my stomach more and more with each passing day.

I remember feeling so lost and alone thinking, *"No, Lord, not this one!!! Out of all the men in my life, he is the one that I gave a portion of my heart to.* Letting someone get close to me in any way is HUGE for me, because of my trust issues. I was not ready to hear the truth that I pushed him to give me and when I finally did, I died inside one more time.

When one comes out of what I have, knowing the lies about what I thought was true and then to learn they were not felt like a thousand blows to my heart. When the foundation of your world is never stabile, it feels like walking on quick sand. My life had been made up of half-truths, broken promises, deception, betrayals, and abuse. At a very young age, any form of security was stripped away from me.

It took me a while to find the right path God wanted me to be on and I am still learning even today. As I pursued God to restore my mental health, I never saw in Scripture that I was to trust just anyone, but Him. What He did say was that I was to *love others* with His love and only He could enable me to do so.

I began to accept the fact that I could forgive my ex-husband, love him from afar in God, and have no contact with him for my own safely and well-being. I finally was able to walk away from him, but it took every ounce of God in me to do so. I had given this man my heart only to have it be discarded as nothing, due to his *willful* choice to not love me, as a man is called by God to care for his wife.

I was able to embrace the truth that I did have the mind of Christ and that I could trust that He did have a plan and purpose for me, (Jeremiah 29:11). I stood on John 14:27 | AMP: *"Peace I leave with you; My [perfect] peace I give to you; not as the world gives do I give to you. Do not let your heart be troubled, nor let it be afraid. [Let My perfect peace calm you in every circumstance and give you courage and strength for every challenge].* This truth did not become real for me easily, because I did not have peace much of the time.

My soul had been tormented with fear, doubt, and unbelief on such deep levels. The reality that I could actually feel complete peace was foreign to me. The only time I remember experiencing that I could were in two Supernatural encounters I had with Jesus.

One was a dream where I was sitting at a Vanity area in my bedroom. I could see a chair with a mirror in front of me, along with an area where my brushes and cosmetics were. I was a young woman and dressed in a long white night gown. I was covering my face and crying uncontrollably. Then, I felt hands upon my shoulders and I was filled with an overwhelming and unexplainable peace.

As I looked up, I could see Jesus in the mirror behind me from the neck down in a white robe. I closed my eyes to embrace His love that was pouring into me. He then bent down and whispered in my ear, *"I died so you would not have to go through this."* The dream ended and I came back to all of my five physical senses.

The next time was when I went through some Spiritual Deliverance and I was working through the pain of another separation with my ex-husband. For a split second and in between me falling asleep, I felt that same peace again. I so wanted it to stay, but it left as quickly as it came. It was unspeakable, breathtaking, and so powerful. I finally understood Philippians 4:7 | NIV: *"And the peace of God, which transcends all understanding, will guard your hearts and your minds in Christ Jesus."*

While my pain has been great, it has always brought me back to Jesus. He continues to give me life lessons to apply in whatever situation I may be facing and He has taught me to live by four truths:

Truth No. 1

What Does God Say? God wants to have an, *"intimate,"* relationship with us. Many do not understand what that means and think it is only in a romantic relationship, but it is not. The truth I needed to believe was what God said about me and not what *others* thought I should be. This helped me press into Him more in seeking only His validation of me in Him. I also learned a lot about legalism and how the enemy uses it to keep one bound.

Jesus saw this in the Sadducees and Pharisees and it was not something that He walked away from either. He took the scriptures they would use to try and trap Him by turning it around into a question about *themselves*. It either left them pondering on what He said or be offended, but Jesus just walked away free as a bird. Why? Because He *knew* the truth.

His truth is not always easy to digest and it is a reality check that many cannot handle even in this day and age. Yet, I wanted to be free from any type of legalism, hypocrisy, or living a mediocre life style. If that meant having very few friends, then so be it, and many times it was just God and I.

I became conscious about others ways and behaviors. If it did not bring peace and unity in God, I went back to what I knew on how relationships ought to be life. Sure, we all have issues and no one is perfect, but when the relationship became unsettling within my spirit, heart, and soul, I knew I needed to do a heart check and retreat in Him.

Just today, I walked away from another friendship that I could see red flags immediately in. I asked God to confirm what I should do and it was like a, *"knowing,"* within me surfaced. I heard these words, *"Go with what you know."* I did, exited gracefully from the relationship trusting that God was speaking to me, and that what I was sensing was of Him. Knowing what God says about things is vital to doing life.

When we know the principles of how He calls us to do relationships in a healthy way and the *opposite* is present in our lives, we have a choice to make. It is in those times that we really need to lean into what God is saying to us and not what our emotions want to dictate us to believe.

Truth No. 2

<u>What Does My Spirit Say</u>? Learning to decipher this truth came with spending intimate time with God and understanding his principles. I was able to compare what I was thinking, (or sensing), with what I knew God's character to be. It helped me not be led astray by emotions, as they are fickle. I was able to see the truth in how I was feeling and how my spirit was being led.

There were times that I thought for sure it was God only to learn that it was not. It caused me to retreat into not being led too much on what I felt or thought. I would pray in tongues, fast, study, and seek counsel just to make sure that I was not being led by demonic voices. In time, I began to trust myself more. When there was a check within me, I needed to take a step back, and allow the Lord to lead me. Compulsivity was not something I could afford in my life.

I remember one time, I was in the kitchen and I was separated from my ex-husband again. He was having an affair and all of the sudden I knew who the other woman was. When I addressed this with him, he could not believe that I had figure it out and that I knew who the woman was beyond a shadow of a doubt.

Then there were times where I would get this prompting within to pray through something in tongues only. When I did, the Holy Spirit would reveal more things that I suspected was going on in my marriage. While it was very hard to walk through, I began to see many of the lies that the enemy had me deceived in. As I partnered more with God, additional discernment came on other things.

At various times, I would sense an uneasiness around certain people. When I pressed into it more, things were revealed about that person's heart motives. I would pray for them to see their need for God in their life, but I would have to lay some boundaries for myself with them in detaching in a healthy way.

Prior to trusting what my spirit was saying, I was led by emotions, fear, manipulation, and control. I knew no other way, as it was how I was raised. In my marriages, I never felt secure enough to trust my instincts. There were too many mind games that existed and it was a form of witchcraft through a mind-binding spirit. I would be certain about one thing and then speak to one of my exs only to be confused again. Then the blame shifting would start and there were no real resolutions to the conflict we were facing.

I think of Eve in the Garden where satan tempted her by causing her to doubt what God had instructed her and Adam to do. It is the oldest trick in the book. However, I always go back to what Adam did when he was questioned by God. He blamed Eve and, *"Passing the buck,"* was born.

Once I began to know the truth in what scripture says, I learned to invite God into the conversation on any issue I was facing. I also was not so gullible in trusting people, unless the fruit of their lives and words *matched* the character of Christ. While I know that no one is perfect, the Holy Spirit taught me how to become a very good Fruit Inspector not only in my own life, but in those around me.

Truth No. 3

<u>What Does the Holy Spirit Say</u>? Learning to ask this questions has come in stages. I did not trust myself and the programming I had within me to discern correctly what I was hearing. As I matured, there were days where I felt God's leading so clearly with some form of direction being dropped within me on what to do. There was a peace and an assurance that came with it also, causing me to stay stress-free and confident in what I was led to do.

To help me understand the Holy Spirit more, I would study about His character and what part He played in the God-Head. I learned that He is the Father's Spirit sent by Jesus to comfort, guide, and counsel us. In John 14:16, He's referred to as our, *"paraclete,"* (our advocate and counselor), and I could truly say I understand that to be true in my life.

There were times where I would be trying to sleep or wake up in the morning, but my mind was all over the place and the Holy Spirit would sooth me. Other times, I would wake up with a song in my heart. When I would listen to the song, it would minster to me in an area that I was struggling in. Sometimes, I would have plans to do something and I would feel a tugging within my heart not to. I later would find out that if I had gone ahead with my plans, it would not have turned out in my favor.

I have also found that there are different ways the enemy attack us – in our sleep, when we are tired, if we are upset, and when we wake up in the morning. It is when he can catch us, *"off guard,"* because our emotions are at their peak. That is when the demonic entities sent to harass us spew their lies into our souls.

It is vital for me now to wake up every morning and invite the Holy Spirit into my day. When I do, life goes so much smoother. At other times, I will get a warning on something by Him. Later on, it is like I am having a, *"Day ja vue,"* moment, because He has given me insight on what is taking place already.

Truth No. 4

<u>Does It Line Up With the Truth of God's Word</u>? When I am triggered, all kinds of emotions rise up within me and I can feel the presence of

evil trying to invade my soul. I finally wanted to know why and I soon learned the answers. Soul wounds. There were numerous areas within me that had been damaged by the enemy through abuse, people, and circumstances. Once set in motion, I was off and running! Yet, I did not know how to stop it from happening or that it was *even* happening.

My past traumas had me believing the worst about people, things, and myself. I was very suspicious and felt like everyone was out to get me. I was becoming so paranoid that I had to figure out how overcome it. I knew that it fed the PTSD and that when I did not have a peace within me that I was to not make a move.

Sometimes I would miss it and then condemnation came in. I would later learn to decipher what conviction from God was versus the condemning voice of the enemy. I had a lot of times that I would just have to wait, stay in peace, and seek the Scriptures out for the answers I needed. For a person like me, that felt like an eternity. I usually was the one who, *"put the cart before the horse,"* because I was on edge most of time.

I wanted to seize the moment when things where good before they went dark again. Needless to say, this put me in some major predicaments that caused me to make some pretty bad life choices. Obviously, it was in the relationships I was in that led me to marry for all the wrong reasons. Not knowing how to seek God's word for direction kept me deceived. I had to learn to be sensitive to what Scripture was saying or whether it was me, the devil, or my triggers talking.

I remember having an encounter with Jesus where He reminded me that I was forgiven and not held accountable for some of the things that I had done. I did not know any better and the wounded parts of me where making decisions that a child would make, because they had never grown up. They were stuck in my past when the abuse occurred and only reacting to the fear they felt. It lead me on the path to finally being able to forgive myself and move into a whole other realm of freedom.

However, it would have never come if I did not become established in understanding the word of God, how to apply it to my life, and to remember that I was to walk by faith and not by sight, as it says in 2 Corinthians 5:7.

11

Keys In Becoming Free

ONE AFTERNOON, I WAS HAVING AN EMDR SESSION WITH MY THERAPIST on the betrayal I felt when I learned of my one of my ex's affairs. God was using these times to reset my soul and I remember feeling a, *"shift,"* in having more peace inside. I began to process other things I had stuffed for years in being married and divorced more than once.

I would weep a lot during those sessions and I hated it when I cried, because I was taught by my abusers to be tough. I had be ridiculed when I showed weakness and the words I remember were, *"You want to cry? I will give you a reason to cry!"* Without me knowing it, I was conditioned to be hard hearted when I saw anyone showing weakness. I began to see that my boldness also drew others to me, especially weak men. Later these men because passive/aggressive and used their ability to abuse me to make up for their own insecurities. While I was bold, I did not have the bodily strength a man does.

The key component that led me to these men was not having the love by a father or other men in my family. They were all distant, insensitive, workaholics, and non-reverential to God. My view of what a man was by these types of role models is what led me to pick men that were broken. Eventually, I faced the fact that I needed a lot more support incorporated into my healing process. I remember praying and sensing the Holy Spirit saying to me that it was not going to be a, *"quick fix,"* either.

Thankfully, God had begun bringing some key people into my life that were my Divine Connections and still are to this day. However, it was difficult in not getting the instant results I wanted. I was remind by the Holy Spirit that I did not get here over night and I was not going to get out overnight either. Was I happy about that? No… It was, (and still is), a process and every day brings something new. Some days are better than others and the ones that are not good are the ones I stay really close to God.

Being an overachiever and perfectionist, the message embedded in me was that I would be punished and suffer some major consequences later, if I did not comply. I equated love with being excellent by how I looked, dressed, gave to others, kept my home, car, or anything pertaining to me. I experienced OCD, if I was not doing all that I thought I should be doing to feel in control. It is a spirit associated with many others that the enemy had used against me.

Insanity was another one and I also had an, *"orphan spirit,"* mentality upon me that resulted from abandonment issues. Then there was me feeling rejected by others, which caused me to believe the lie that I was not enough. All the abuse I endured was meant to tear down my very being and who God had created me to be. Each of the soul wounds I faced had some form of demonic influence attached to it giving them legal access to torment me.

Unknowingly, this created my deep need to be valued in I became performance-based. I later saw that these mindsets gave me a narcissistic mentality in being the center of attention. I remember one of my exs labeling me this personality type and I did not understand it back them. Although he would never admit it to me, he was one to. Satan is the first narcissist, so this is one of the main areas he afflicts people with.

God took me on some interesting encounters in sharing why they existed in me and how to remove them from my life. I pressed into my studies, praying, going to therapy, seeking balanced coaching, and counseling from my Divine Connections. Eventually, change started to take place and I also learned that the key to my overcoming was learning to surrender it all to God *wholeheartedly.*

Surrendering Food to God

They were numerous times, (and still are), where I have had to do this in my life. When I began to peel away the layers of my abuse, I did not know how I was still standing in the natural. I have lived on auto-pilot for so long that it became a pattern to use food as my comfort. Food did not talk back, was there when I needed it to be, and kept me in a comatose state of mind after binging on sugar, fried foods, and lots of carbs.

Connecting to all my shattered parts when I would disassociate was overwhelming also. It was another reason I would eat and I exhausted all of my head knowledge in trying to fix me. Despite the countless diets I tried, none of them worked in healing my broken self-image. I finally had to accept that I could not do it alone. This eating disorder that plagued me had to be addressed, as I definitely was not in my right mind when it came to food.

First, I acknowledged that there was a food addiction that fed me when I was happy, sad, mad, or whatever my state of mind may have been on any particular day. Being raised in a Latin family did not always help either, because a lot of things revolved around food. My mother was notorious for making sure we ate. If we did not, the lectures came on how important it was to do so, especially breakfast.

I am still having to surrender not eating when I am triggered and it is a daily conscious effort to stay on track and some days are better than others. I can literally consume so much food at one time and then feel completely ugly, fat, condemned, and guilty afterwards. I am sure some of you reading this can relate to what I am sharing. If I let it, it becomes a vicious cycle that repeats itself making me so sick and tired of being *literally* sick and tired.

The weight issues caused me to become very disturbed with how I looked, felt, and even dressed. Medical terminology refers to it as Body Dysmorphic Disorder, (BDD), where I see myself as, *"frumpy,"* even though everyone else would call me, *"Beautiful."* The problem was that I did not see myself that way and would go right back to food as my comfort.

I also learned that many SRA Survivors struggle with food issues. For control and manipulation, SRA perpetrators starve their victims or cause them to eat and drink unspeakable things. When we get out of cult rituals, eating regular food can become an obsession. For me, it is even more so, especially when COVID-19 hit. Having been isolated so much, depression was loosed over our world and has caused many to become overweight.

Food addiction is also something that runs in my family lineage. We are either full-figured or anorexic. In my case, I would put on weight in hopes that it would deter me from being sexually abused or that the men I was married to would stop being attracted me. It did not, because sexual addiction is ruled by lust and it is a very diabolical mindset to overcome. Realizing that the men in my life had issues in this area way before I came into the picture has helped me see that I am not the one with the problem.

Understanding How to Heal the Soul

In 2016, I learned about how to heal soul wounds and I was immediately drawn to finding out what it was all about. I saturated myself with teachings on the subject and learned about Deliverance Prayers that caused my soul and heart to heal faster. The way I had been programmed to believe began to change finally. Then I got connected to a few Facebook On-line Communities and to get support with others. I was led to connect with those who have or were walking in my shoes with food addiction, along with healing from SRA, anxiety, and depression.

I learned to see how the foods I was eating contributed to many of my ailments. I started to make healthier choices by eliminating the toxins I had been feeding my body for years, but there was one problem – I did not know how to stop overeating when I was not hungry.

As my soul continues to heal, my writings are also beginning to change. I am purposing to see myself differently, so that I can begin doing life in a healthier way. I have had to retrain my default mechanisms to go to God, instead of addictions. I have had to make conscious choices about toxic relationships being part of my life to, because many of them were with Food Addicts.

In other relationships, I have had to release all bitterness and resentment with a purpose to forgive. I try to remember that I have been forgiven of much, but it is still a process. Doing this does not mean I go and have Tea with those who have harmed me either. It does mean that I am to pray for them when everything in me wants to retaliate.

When challenges come, I get into my Quiet Time before the Lord and remind myself that I need to surrender it all to Him. Has it been easy? No, but well worth it in the end, as I continue to allow the Holy Spirit to cleanse my heart and soul.

Those are really heavy loads to carry and they only breed poisons inside of me. I am not hurting anyone, but myself either when I hold on to them. I have heard it said like this, *"Unforgiveness is like drinking poison expecting it to harm the person who has hurt us."* Reality check for sure!

Transitioning Into Health

Have you ever wanted something to happen, (even dreamed of it for years), but it did not? Welcome to my world! I was the greatest at having a desire for something to change or implement a new idea. Yet, I struggled in sticking to a game plan to have it take place.

There was a large amount of disappointment, procrastination, and negative self-talk that sabotaged me right out of what I wanted for my life. I would end up settling for less, because I felt like I did not deserved any better. The life I had led taught me that I was not good enough and it took me coming to terms with how I saw myself physically.

It is a well-known fact that many people during the COVID pandemic got really, let us just say, *"plump."* For the first time in my life, I fit right into society and was not the minority, but the majority. Being big was becoming more accepted and made it easier for me to not feel like such an outcast anymore. Plus, change did not come easy for me. I was use to routine, structure, and doing things that I know I can do well. I had to transition into not living in a survival mode all the time.

Now, I seek to have a life-style that is simple, stress-free, and orderly. When it does not go that way, there is a lot of triggering within me taking place. I often wish I could have a man's brain in this area. When you ask him what he is thinking and he replies, *"Nothing,"* he literally means it! My brain was use to processing too much information all at once.

I have since learned that my mind has groves imbedded in it from past traumas, addictions, and abuses, which has programmed me on how to think. The flip side of that is that I have the ability to reprogram myself or as Scriptures says, *"renew my mind."* God has created us so intricately that the brain and body can actually heal itself when it operates the way it was created to.

The one thing I have noticed about myself is that learning how to implement change can be easy, if it is something I want or like to do. Dysfunctional thinking says, *"It is easier to stay stuck and miserable, because that is been my life."* Then there is the side of me that wants more and desires to change completely.

I am taking it one day at a time, along with staying close to God to be balanced. My identity has been wrapped around so many faulty mindsets, programs, and lies, but I am not giving up hope on becoming all that God has created me to be.

Finding Me

God is continually reminding me on having healthy boundaries and not to try to be in control of everything. Purposing to use wisdom in not making the same mistakes I have made before is the path I chose to stay on. At times I succeed and at other times I do not. One key factor is that I do not allow just anyone into my inner circle anymore.

Before, I trusted too quickly or married men who I saw had, *"potential,"* because I believed in them more than they believed in themselves. I finally decided to do that for *myself* in learning to see my potential in God. I am learning to have a new perspective and to lean on His direction and not my own. I have also begun to see people differently and that things are not always the way they look.

Where I used to be judgmental and critical, God has changed my heart to see beyond the actions people make into seeing their heart motives instead. He often shows me the spirit behind the person and where the enemy is working through them. He is teaching me that not everyone is for me although I may want them to be. Trusting myself to discern other's characters is also something I am using more wisdom on. I am being more mindful and intuitive of the plots and plans of the enemy and trusting God as my safety net in all things.

God also keeps taking me on a journey of learning what Heaven and Hell are really about. He is giving me discernment on seeing the demonic things that are taking place, but also the heavenly things that are to. Being wise in not allowing my emotions to dictate my life has taught me much too. I have had to, *"woman up,"* (so to speak), and learn to manage my emotions far more than I use to.

Finding the new me had already given me some tools, but I still did not trust myself fully in using them. There were parts of me that connected to people's unhealthy ways of doing life, because that felt normal to me. I had to deal with parts of me that were not happy, which challenged me regularly. I have definitely grown and the old me is continually healing, maturing, and learning about my gifts, talents, passions in life, and so much more.

I am not where I use to be and I am so grateful for that. I learned that becoming my own best friend was the most important decision I ever made in my life. The next decision was learning what abuse was all about, identifying it, and getting it out of in my life for good.

12

Seven Types of Abuse

IT WAS AN UNEXPECTED BLOW TO MY FACE THAT I DID NOT SEE COMING from my second ex-husband. We were separated and he had been stalking me for years. On this particular day, he had come to my home to get back the wedding ring he had given to me. It was a sizeable one worth much and I was not prepared for how far he would go to get it back. He literally punched me in the face right in front of my daughter, who was about 10-years old at the time.

I no longer was in shock from the blow, but filled with pure rage at the audacity of this man doing this in MY home and in FRONT of my daughter. I rose to my feet quickly to stop him from going into my bedroom. Then he took another punch, but this time it was to my stomach knocking the wind out of me. I flew across the room hitting my back up against the kitchen counter, while my daughter screamed from the top of her lungs for help.

Even though many could hear the abuse going on, the lack of care that our neighbors had for us was so disturbing to me. This time, I called the Police and went through the embarrassment of reporting the abuse that had taken place. My eyes were left black and blue, along with having a bloody nose. My lungs were bruised making it hard to breath and I had a huge knot on the back of my head.

I was traumatized beyond words, my apartment was torn up in him trying to get my ring, (which he could not find), and I cried all night holding my daughter. All I kept thinking was me having to get up in the morning to go to work and how I was going to cover up the bruising to my face the next day. It was a new job and could not afford to take off work.

I have no clue how I made it to work. Immediately, my co-worker saw that something was wrong. I shared with them what had happened in confidence, but they shared it with my management anyways. That afternoon, I was let me go with my Supervisor claiming that she did not feel I could perform the job they hired me for with my, *"personal issues."* There was no concern for me and my safety either. Sadly, this had happened to me with other positions and it was getting harder to sustain a job. My fears of how I was going to provide for me and my child plagued me day and night.

Until later in life, I did not know that there was more than one type of abuse. I thought that it came only in the form of being, *"physical,"* abused and many still do today. The men in my own family did not see Domestic Violence this way either, because they saw no physical evidence that I was being hit. I was also so brainwashed that I did not think I was being raped by my second ex-husband either, because *"I was married,"* to him. How wrong I was. I also had a love/hate relationship with myself, because I picked these men who had no clue what love was, but then again neither did I.

Sadly, I have literally walked in every one of the seven types of abuses explained below. It caused me to not be able to experience what trust was with others in any of these areas. As a woman, it kept me feeling broken in all the other areas of my life as well, but I have learned a few things since then that I want to pass on to you.

The Seven Types of Abuse

1. Physical: Growing up, I witnessed my siblings and mother beaten repeatedly. Viewing my own family trying to kill each other was brutal to me mentally growing up. I've continued to

heal from being triggered at hearing raised voices, loud crashing sounds, and any kind of violence near me. My mother had to cut off her beautiful long black hair to avoid being dragged on the floor by it when she and my father would fight.

This taught me and my siblings to take anything we could get our hands on to hurt one another when we would fight. I distinctly remember one time when my brother and sister had a horrible fight. My brother took a spray can of something, threw it at my sister, and it caused her to have a deep wound about an inch long on her forehead that left her scarred for life. When he saw what he had done, he ran frantically out of the room. I was the one left to clean up the bloody mess and get help for my sister.

Then there were the welt lashes on my siblings backs when they were hit by our father with his own belt that I cringed at seeing. The reality of how rage ran within our home kept me in a state of sheer fear.

2. Sexual: The worst abuse I endured was this one not only through the SRA, but as a wife. Pornography and a heavy spirit of lust was always present in my marriages and it damaged me greatly. I was asked to do what was seen in these types of abnormal sexual encounters.

When I would not perform the degrading acts that were required of me, my punishment came afterwards. I was rejected, verbally shamed, mocked, or denied any closeness whatsoever. Then there were the affairs to replace me, which only defiled our marriage bed even more.

Due to these issues not being treated in my exs, their addictions got worse and more demanding wounding me more inside. I learned, (the hard way), that nothing could satisfy sexual desires when dealing with Sex Addicts, (SAs) or Porn Addicts, (PAs). That is what they saw or learned from their fathers, other family members, or friends, and some of them were even molested themselves.

As I studied Spiritual Deliverance, there are sexual spirits that enter when one is subjected to sexual addictions, satanism, witchcraft, or cult practices. They have various names, such as, *"marine demons"* and *"spirit spouses,"* in the family of the, incubus and succubus spirits. Due to my abuse, they were transferred to me and cast out later, thankfully. These spirits come at night through one's dreams and actually have intercourse with a person. They also cause someone to not want to be with their mates intimately.

3. Spiritual: I endured this type of abuse with various churches by those in ministry positions using their authority against me. When I reported two of my exs to Church Leadership, they believed the lies told them about me. We were basically written off, (especially me), when I refused to be labeled as the one with all the issues.

There were numerous counseling sessions and I usually was given the same advice. As long as any of my exs were willing to do the work to salvage the marriage, I needed to, *"submit,"* to my husband, because God hates divorce. If I did divorce, I could not be used in ministry either. Little did they know what was going on behind closed doors and that God cared more about *me* being safe than the institution of marriage.

The spirit of an addict/abuser lies, controls, and manipulates well, with a Doctor Jekyll/Mr. Hyde personality that inhabits passive/aggressive behaviors. The men in my life were all Intimacy Anorexics, (IAs), who purposely withheld from me love, affection, attention, and had very little empathy. They also had issues with their mothers and women in general. It caused them to be, *"misogynist,"* (someone who hates women and are prejudiced again them).

This left me feeling like I was living in a prison within my own home. I ended up becoming an IA to self-protect and detach from the abuse I was in. Then there was the continual blame shifting and gas lighting going on. This is where I was blamed for pretty much everything, could not do anything right for too long, and was made out to be the bad one, while my addict/abuser was portrayed and viewed as the, *"victim."*

4. <u>Financial</u>: There was such a control over the finances and I was kept under my exs thumbs. I was ill from all of the betrayals, control, fighting, and deception that I could not earn a steady income, which put me at my abusers mercy. I continued to lose cars, homes, jobs, and my sanity, along with being stripped of any self-worth or dignity. I felt emotionally drained and in a zombie type of mindset half of the time.

This led me to become co-dependent on my addict/abusers, which enabled them to manipulate my every move and that is the way they liked it. They also had their own separate Savings and Checking Accounts. When I did join my accounts with them, I would then be abused by funds I earned being take out for themselves causing division, lack of trust, us having a, *"Contract Marriage,"* and they wanted everything to be 50/50.

Each time we parted ways, others or my precious mother would end up coming in to give me funds to buy a car, get into a place to live, have food, and put cloths on my back. After every marriage, I had begun to rebuild my life again, regain my voice, and identity to start a new, but it was so taxing on my mental and physical health.

5. <u>Verbal</u>: I have experienced being called a, *"Cow, prude, frigid, callous, and an emotionally unstable person,"* by the men that claimed to love me. This type of abuse is pretty much accepted by society nowadays dismissing others feelings easily. There is little value on being treated decently or with respect. This was another form of psychological manipulation, causing me to question my own purpose and stripping me of having any confidence in myself.

Addict/abusers sexual addictions cause them to become like a drug addict who want their fixes whenever, wherever, and with whomever they can use. In their eyes, I was no longer seen as a person, but as an, *"object,"* and spoken to as one. When I would give into their demands, I was left feeling discarded like an old Raggedy Ann Doll. One minute I was loved by them and the next minute, I was torn up by their brutal words.

6. <u>Emotional</u>: This abuse is how I was kept from running for help. I was initially groomed into trusting my exs and then, like a venous snake, they would strike out and poison me with their abuse leaving me for dead. I constantly doubted myself when I would question any porn found, suspected affairs, and asked why they were coming in so late from work. It was turned around as, *"my issue,"* that I was being a, *"nag,"* and paranoid, so the focus was taken off of them and put on me.

   I could even prove that they were either having an affair, lying, or doing porn, and it was still dismissed or minimized. This entailed hours of arguing and never getting a straight answer to anything. I was then the one who was, *"bi-polar"* or *"narcissistic."*

   I would leave and stay with others to regain my sanity, but ignorantly returned later. Feeling so ashamed to be living in these types of situations more than once left me not wanting to share too much with others. My exs also did not fail to remind me that the reasons why my other marriages failed were because of, *"me."*

   While I was the common denominator in all of my relationships, it was not because I wanted to be. I was wounded and trapped in the vicious cycle of abuse that stripped me from having any peace or stability. I so wanted to be loved only to be abused and blamed, even by my family, friends, and the church. It has taken a lot of repenting for putting others before God, many nights of processing, lots of tears shed, years of forgiving others, (including myself), and extensive therapy to recover.

7. <u>Mental</u>: This was when I was subjected to so many, *"mind games,"* of being loved one day and hated the next. There were times that I would try to engage with my exs to get help and was led to believe that they would. I would later find out that they were not truly committed to the process and still engaging in their addictions or affairs. It took its mental toil on me to try and keep the truth from lies separated.

   I truly wanted to believe that they were doing the right thing by me, our families, themselves, and especially God. To only find out that it was all a lie was far more than I could take at times. It sent me continually into a dark place that I became suicidal at various times.

When I would separate myself from my exs, the darkness began to lift and I was able to regain some form of focus. The long journey of healing my soul and finding out what mental health was psychologically and spiritually finally began. Thankfully, God has been faithful in helping me learn about the disorders I dealt with and how to overcome them.

Abuser/Victim Mentality

Although I was raised in abuse, throughout my life I never knew that I was in an abusive relationship, until I started to get healthy. I began to learn about boundaries, using my voice, getting help to protect myself, and staying true to me. These things are unheard of when you live in abuse.

You are taught to stay silent, pretend, deny, and make excuses to what you are being subjected to. The hardest thing for a victim of abuse to do is deal with their own reality, because an abused person has been trained to take the blame for things that were not their fault in the first place.

Another thing one learns to do is question themselves on *everything.* My addict/abusers had a way of making me think that I was insane, causing me to continually think I was. It all stemmed from being told that I was, *"emotionally unstable."* I could not identify the very high walls erected within me and I did not know how to break them down without help.

Living in my abuse numbed me from the reality that this *was not* normal. It paralyzed me from thinking that I could have a happy life, so I learned to endure and cope in the midst of it all. I mirrored my abusers behaviors of being angry, stubborn, unreasonable, demanding, narcissistic, prideful, and controlling. As I got free from each one of my abusive relationships, I was triggered a lot when people would try to overpower me.

Yet, I needed to be needed or accepted, so I tried to buy people's friendships or love. Now, I can see the signs of an abusive relationship whenever I hear a woman minimize her situation, justify her addict/ abusers ways, and deny that her problems are, *"serious."* When someone cannot be themselves around those who claim to love them, (because they fear their reactions), there *is* something wrong.

If a person cannot go anywhere without another's approval or fears more what others will think than what is best for them, there *is* a problem. When a woman fears for the safety of herself and her children that she avoids standing up for what is right, she is *definitely* in an abusive situation. This is where we are being ruled by fear, intimidation, control, deception, and threats.

In the state of mind I was in, it was easy for someone to cut me off from anyone who could possible influence me in a positive way. I was usually charmed at first to woo me into a relationship. Once I entered into being exclusive, the abuse would begin subtly. There were times of happiness and then there were times of sadness. Eventually, the sadness was ruled by the abusive behavior patterns that would surface.

My abuse did not only come from just men either. There were also destructive relationships with women that I experienced. Some of the worst relationships were with those women in whom I confided in. What I shared in private was then taken and broadcasted to others, even those in the church. I found that although much of my trauma stemmed from my male connections, women can be just as much of an abuser than men.

I would encourage anyone reading this to ask yourself some challenging questions to determine if you are in a toxic or abusive relationship. I was once seeing a Therapist that said for me to run from my second husband for she feared I would end up dead. After several brutal beatings and rapes, I finally broke free. If you see any signs of what I have just described, please seek help. Whatever you do, <u>do not stay silent.</u>

Abuse Is Taught Not Caught

I did not come into this world with the violence, self-centeredness, and selfishness associated with abuse. These behaviors were inherited by what I was raised in. Much of what I experienced came from my parents being exposed to it by their parents inflicting abuse on them, who then passed it down to others. I knew I wanted it to stop with me, so that it would not go from generation-to-generation in my lineage.

I was taught very young to not, *"rock the boat,"* around my parents, siblings, and men. Fear was predominately the major force that programmed me – fear of saying something wrong, fear of being in the wrong place at the wrong time, fear of upsetting others, and most of all – *fear of standing up for myself.* Why? Because when I did try to protect myself, the consequences for it were high.

In suppressing my feelings, I grew up a very angry child filled with lots of rage. I became the high school bully, because I had been treated that way by family and others. All those years of never being able to defend myself from being abused came out later in one form or another of rage. Yet deep inside, I felt so helpless and had no outlet.

My self-esteem was so low that I saw no value or worth in who I was, but only in what I *did*. Doing life this way caused me to be very unhealthy in how I parented my own child. I related to others by repeating the same pattern I saw my parents live in. Feeling unwanted caused more rejection and I would work, (to the point of exhaustion), to prove that I was worth something.

These faulty ways of thinking and feeling about myself led me to smoking, compulsivity, and abusing others without even knowing what I was doing. It severed relationships with my family and having real friends was unheard of. I also was taught to never show that I was weak, despite there being so many fears deep within my heart and soul.

I wore masks for everything in my life, never truly allowing myself to feel or be really known. I smiled, pretended, and worst of all, *"played church,"* for far too long. I became critical, judgmental, and opinionated of everything and everyone. I was bitter, resentful, and full of negativity. Worst of all, I hated myself for who I had become that I sabotaged myself from being whole.

I lost all empathy and compassion for anyone in pain. My thought pattern was, *"If I had gone through so much and survived, so could they."* Pride reigned heavily within me, never allowing me to be able to say I was wrong or apologize. It was a way of being that protected my heart from becoming soft and letting anyone too close. Yet, I really was just a wounded and broken woman looking for approval, love, and acceptance.

Then there was the other side of me that was overly responsible for everyone's feelings and wished that others would be that way towards me. Yet, no one in my family was, so I became a very co-dependent caretaker to anyone who knew me. I would get angry that I was this way and it became a twisted way of thinking, which led to self-hatred.

Not having a real childhood in order to help my mother run the house, pay the bills, and so much more left me unbalanced in who I was. There was no understanding why I felt the way I did and there was no one to guide me through my pain. My life consisted of feeling so misunderstood by many. The labels given to me by my past poor choices did not come off that easily, but I was determined to overcome them.

Tools to Surviving Abuse

While my story of abuse, (and countless others), may be something that is becoming way too common these days, it does not have to all end poorly. I cannot say that it will be easy to recover from abuse, but it is *absolutely* possible. When I finally started to, it freed me up to consciously not be abused or to abuse others by purposely reprogramming my brain continually and though processes.

All the old dysfunction imprints had to be erased and God led me to some amazing people in overcoming the mentality of being an, *"Abuse Survivor."* I wanted my past not to be remembered as this, but as someone who had the ability to be victorious. It took me to a place of seeing myself in a whole different way than I had before.

It identifies me with freedom, change, and growth. It helps me see that in the midst of abuse, life *can* change. If I did my part to heal and have healthy boundaries for myself, then things would naturally fall in place, even if it did not always turn out the way I wanted or when I wanted. True change did occur, as I put my effort into changing *me*. I could not do anything about the addict/abusers in my life, (as they did not care to change), but what I could do was separate myself from them permanently.

As I began to get stronger, I was finally able to walk away from each marriage and I also did the unthinkable – I began to call the Police and file Restraining Orders to protect me and my family. I also reported any molestations of family members and others to the Police. This was HUGE for me to do, but I did not want my perpetrators to continue hurting anyone else.

As my mother would always say, *"It takes two to tangle,"* and if one is not willing to get help, then the other person can only release them and move on. I prayed a lot for the men in my life and I have mourned for them to. How they chose to live their lives left a bloody trail of heartache.

The next step I purposed to do was to get medically treated for the issues I was facing. I fought for my sanity and began dealing with all the infirmities I had. This is what living in abuse does to a person and many do not even connect the two. I listened to experts in the health industry and each ailment was attached to some form of mental instability or stress that was manifesting in parts of my body.

Despite my lack of trust, I forced myself to get involved in support groups with those who were on the same road I was on in getting better. Once I began to finally take care of myself, I saw that God had given me so much to give back to others in the midst of my pain. He continues to redeem what was once a very dark part of my life and I am still learning. Is my life perfect? No. Yet, I still believing that He will turn it into something beautiful.

I finally had to come to a place of no longer begging others, (especially my abusers), to love me back. It took a lot of work to no longer seek anything from them. I am learning daily to seek my validation from God and not others perceptions or opinions of me.

How I was *taught* formed why I made many of the life choices I did. When one does not know anything else and they are isolated from the world or so programmed by dysfunctional thinking, it is very challenging to know how or what to believe. I know for me it was and I am still deprogramming the lies that were put into me regularly.

13

The Process of Healing

❖ ❖ ❖

I WAS 25-YEARS OLD AND WORKING AT MY DREAM JOB. I HAD ALREADY gone through one divorce, but my career was going well. My only child was 5-years old and I was having a hard time accepting the fact that I was a single parent. I remember trying to get out of the house to be at work on time, but I still had to leave my child at daycare.

I arrived at work stressed, out of breath, and fearful that I would be late. My Supervisors where very good to me, but I lived in constant anxiety in being on time to work. Life was hard not only for me, but also for my child too. Being put in the position I was by her father leaving me pregnant at 19 for another woman caused much resentment within me.

It finally hit me on that day – my world was not going to be easy and I had better learn to deal with it. I still felt like I was a little girl inside myself wanting to be cared for and safe. My upbringing had stunted my growth process and that would not change, until I faced working through the traumas of where I had come from.

I had no clue what it was to be treated like a woman was to be in God's eyes. My parents never truly understood what their upbringing did to me. Until later, I would not comprehend that my own parents were wounded just as much as they wounded me. They also had no role models in their own lives to know how to raise healthy children.

As a toddler, my innocence had been stripped from me leaving me feeling so uncomfortable in my own skin and I was the odd ball in group settings later on in life. Growing up, I was strong, bold, outspoken, and somewhat of a Tom Boy, which later changed. I found my worth in beauty and fashion, but it still did not change the broken image I had inside about me. Then there was the SRA that took place from ages 10 to 17 that really affected me. By the time I was 19, living in abuse is all I knew.

I taught my abusers to treat me poorly by *allowing* it. Sadly, I cannot even remember a time growing up that I witnessed anyone being truly valued in my surrounding relationships. To keep the peace when abusing or cheating on my mother, my father would bring home flowers and candy to calm things down. That only lasted so long, until the next outburst would take place between them.

I was afraid of my parents and could not voice it, so I learned to, *"stuff it."* It seemed like every environment I was in was controlled with rage, abuse, manipulation, and denial. Then there was the, *"white elephant,"* in the middle of the room that no one wanted to address, accept me. I was looked upon as being too cocky, bold, bossy, and strong-willed, but mainly angry.

I wanted to be accepted for me, but my childhood was filled with so much misguided direction on love, life, and my identity. It was where the, *"perfectionist,"* in me was born, which caused me to only be more lost in knowing who I really was. I became performance oriented and based things on what I did and not on who I was in God. All of these things led me to become so discontent with life, which then forced me to face my world with a HUGE, *"reality check."*

Dealing With Rejection and Abandonment

In my brief time with my father, I did not bond with him the way a child should and can only recall one memory with him when I was a toddler. I was afraid on something that had just happened to me. I went to him crying and he sat me down on his lap and tried to comfort me to the best of his ability. That was it – that was the extent of me remembering any form of connection with him. I also remember the smell of alcohol and cigarettes on his breath.

My mother was a woman of strength and passion. Yet, it was channeled wrongly, due to the areas of her many soul wounds. Her childhood and her marriage to my father had severely damaged her in many ways. She became like many women are today who endure hard times – they learned to *survive* at all costs.

She had the strength to make it, until she could not anymore. In her own unique way, she loved God. Later in life, she became lost in her pain and that came out through dominance, control, rage, bitterness, and unforgiveness. As a child, my mother had been rejected and abandoned. Those seeds grew deep within her, which was then passed down to her children in her mothering. I do not think she did intentionally, but knew no other way to be. I was the only one who would eventually understand her, which is why I remained her Caretaker from my teens to adulthood, until she crossed over.

I had seen the same pattern with men in my mother's life. My own personal rejection and abandonment were reinforced every time I married an unhealthy man. I grew more fragile in my heart with their rejection of my deep need to be secure. It was the same pattern – they would physically leave or stay in the marriage, but detach due to their infidelity, drug, alcohol, or porn addiction.

Yet, every man I was with regretted not preserving our relationship afterwards. Despite my flaws, my heart to love them was pure. I did so in being nurturing, caring, and bringing them the support that I so desperately needed. I gave to them what I wish I could have *from them*.

I fought hard to make things work, but, it was like God would somehow intervene to make it impossible for me to stay with them or they would leave me. The abandonment and rejection still plagued me though. My life consisted of usually waiting in fear wondering when it would get worse. The feeling I would get when I was struck with panic or anxiety was unspeakable and my mind would go into a state of confusion.

As I continued trying to find answers to the many questions that I had about my life, I learned what, *"evil foreboding,"* was about. It was a demonic attack to my soul that kept me in a tail spin of dread, doubt, unbelief, and negativity with the presence of evil lingering. When I was in this mindset, peace was incomprehensible.

I remember hearing a message about one woman's negative attitude and why she had it. She spoke about feeling that if she believed that nothing good would happen, then she would not be disappointed. Yet, she felt like she had given *"legal access,"* for the evil foreboding to enter in by how her mindset was. The enemy would send his demonic voices to torment her soul and she did not know how to stop it. To her, it was normal for her to hear and think as she did, until she became a Christian. I saw my life in hers so clearly and the light began to turn on in what I was facing personally.

I then began learning about Spiritual Warfare, inner healing, and deliverance. I also knew that, because of what I was exposed to in being ritualistically abused as a child, I had insight on the devil's schemes more than others as well. This only made his attack on my destiny not being fulfilled even more massive.

Where Did I End and Others Begin?

My identity was so warped that I felt like Sally Fields in the movie, *Sybil*, with multiple personalities. All I knew is that some severe abuse had taken place in my past that I had blocked out. I ran from reality by being what others wanted me to be, (instead of the real me), whoever that was.

My mother was the main person that I had not learned to detach from, until she passed away. I was so enmeshed in caring for her that I did not know where I began and she ended. Once my mother passed away, I was face with the need to learn a whole new way of life. It was just me and God to sort things out and it was both a relief and a challenge. I never had been able to just care for, *"me,"* as there was always a person, child, husband, or job that I was responsible for.

I was gifted in various areas at work, so that came easy for me. Yet, I still did not know how to stop seeking approval from people. My background taught me that my validation was based on my *performance*. When I would let myself remotely be who my core person was, I would speak up about things that others only would think about saying. There was much misunderstanding, labeling, judging, criticizing or being shunned that would take place, causing my heart to become more distant.

It came to a point that I did not trust myself to love anyone in a healthy way, (let alone me), so it pushed me more into finding out what love in God was all about. I had such a desire that burned within me to know why I was who I was and then to help others along the way. This is what led me to begin studying Stress Relief Life Coaching.

I also began to learn about the prophetic, along with what God said on having spiritual encounters with Him. It was a world I was able to embrace and was intrigued by all that it entailed. I began to learn that our words have power, we are made in the image of God, and everything that comes forth in the natural realm is *first* birthed in the spiritual realm. It was the connection I needed to accept who God had created me to be spiritually and it released me into a supernatural realm that I was at home in.

It was there that I found myself more, but my relationships with family and men had a long way to go in being truly healed. As I began to peel the layers back, God taught me that He is the only one that knows a person's heart. I could not change anyone other than myself, so that is what I set out to do. I began to look differently at the spiritual and physical realms I lived in. I purposed to declare my promises from the Word of God speaking life into me and my spirit to build my faith. Finally, I was able to overcome the demonic oppressors and pessimistic mindsets I had been programmed to accept.

The journey is still going on today and is a never ending one, but it has revolutionized my world. I have been dramatically changed in my perspectives and that has led me to come a long way from where I was in my former years. As challenging as my life struggles have been, I am now equipped to share my Life Story in hopes of helping others learn from the mistakes I made.

A couple of my life mottos are, *"This too shall pass,"* because, *"Delays do not mean the denial,"* in God's plans and purposes for someone's life. It is all used as stepping stones to the paths He wants us on, which is why I always say that, *"God Doesn't Waste A Hurt,"* (GDWAH). However, before I could fully walk this out in my life, I had to face my past and learn to forgive myself and others.

Understanding my Upbringing

One of my exs would always say this phrase, *"Hind sight is 20/20,"* and I really never understood what that meant, until now. Until much later, understanding why I was raised as I had been did not come to me. I was so performance-based, because my parents were driven in this way. My father was a successful businessman and so were other family members, but the women were broken. Unfortunately, there was little respect by the males for us and we were treated very dishonorably.

What the men in our family failed to realize is that each and every woman in my lineage had much courage, strength, and *tolerance* given to them to endure staying in loveless marriages. We loved deeply and with our full hearts, but we were unheard and uncared for properly.

Sure there were the houses, cars, and families to raise, but there was no, *"connection,"* between husbands and wives. There was also being financial abused attached to all of it, as the women did not work and were basically told to, *"Stay in the kitchen where we belonged!"* The men ruled and reigned like the kings they never really were and lived freely doing as they pleased, when they pleased, with whom they pleased, and with no questions asked.

In our families, children were, *"seen and not heard,"* and we were physically abused with no ability to say a word in retaliation. We were forced to attend Catholic Church and had a mixture of legalism and living a double life style within our homes. The men were addict/abusers, adulterers, and prideful down to my great grandfathers. The women stayed and endured baring several children and much heartache. My own grandmother on my mother's side had 17 children, was severely beaten, and emotionally abused, (along with the kids), by my grandfather.

My upbringing was, *"old school,"* and we did things by the book in staying with an abuser/addict, (no matter what), because we were married. Divorce was frowned upon, which only made me stick out like a sore thumb, since I went through more than one.

When I began to find my voice again, I questioned things, rose up in my convictions, and refused to tolerate living a lie by being in an abusive marriage any longer than I needed to be. When all was said and done, I would have to face the fact that I had done all I could and move on. Did it hurt? Of course it did, but I grew tired of staying in a prison. Change had to talk place or I would literally have killed myself.

Healing Begins

At 50, I went back to school to receive my credentials in mental health and in my studies I saw ME on every page I read! I was sick. I was broken. I was chronically depressed. I was lost. I was in desperate need of a breakthrough. Yet, I loved God and felt a call on my life, despite what it had been up until that point.

I used my training to begin to help my mother heal, (along with myself), and at the time of her crossing over, she had improved much in her remaining years with me. She learned to deal with her unforgiving heart towards the family. She purposed to love God more in a deeper way. She grew in her relationship with me and we healed, as a mother and daughter. I did the best I could in trying to make sure she felt loved and cared for. I gave to her what no one had given to me up to that point in my life. Loving her past her pain taught me how to, *"love well,"* despite the abuse I had gone through in being her child.

In the extra time I spent with her prior to her passing, I could see that I was her in more ways than one and it gave me a HUGE reality check. I had walked in her shoes down to being married and divorced more than once to carrying all the ailments and sicknesses she did. I had no clue how emotionally intertwined I was with her.

During my time in caring for my mother, I had come out of a brutal separation to one of my exs. It literally almost killed me and I went into an emotional breakdown being tormented day and night. My mother was affected by all of this and she grew sicker herself. Sadly, the beginning stages of both Dementia and Alzheimer began to settle into her soul.

I knew that these diseases came in through deep trauma and soul wounds, along with poor health and my mother had them all. My life as it was became too much for her to see me go through. To not be the family she had hoped she would have in me being married and growing old together with her and my mate was something that left her so distraught inside.

We went downhill quickly, until the day I began the tough decision to not die. Prior to that, I had lost my will to even live anymore. The only thing that kept me going was having to care for my mother. In my physical healings, I chose not to go through the conventional way of treating my ailments, but through much prayer and lifestyle changes.

I have grown so much from where I once was and at the time of this writing, I am being well cared for personally by God. I am also staying in my temporary Safe Haven to continue my healing process and produce more books. I am so grateful for being able to pay it forward in sharing with others my story. My writings have been in the makings for several years now. Thankfully, I am finally in a position to focus on them and having to take care of no one, but myself. What a concept!

To be able to achieve healing, I had to learn about abuse, how to be free from it, purpose to get healthy from the inside out, and began to realize that God had so much more for me. A life of abuse is not what He ever wanted us to live. Jesus paid the price for every type of abuse on the Cross *once and for all*. It is time for women everywhere to find themselves and get their voices back by learning what *not* to tolerate in their relationships.

14

God Doesn't Waste a Hurt, (GDWAH)

THIS IS MY VICTORY CHAPTER AND WILL PROBABLY BE THE LONGEST out of the whole book. My past has taught me some very valuable lessons and I have seen countless women, who have been caught in the vicious cycle of abuse. I have encountered every type from all over the world living in abuse. Some still remain in those relationships, others break free, or have been *actually* killed by their abusers.

Then there are those who have literally died emotionally, spiritually, and physically, due to the sicknesses caused by their abuse bringing them to their early deaths. Sadly, my mother was one of them. She never truly healed physically from the beatings she experienced in her marriage to my father. Not to mention her mental and emotional state from the traumas she went though also.

So many marriages and families are destroyed, because of workaholism and addictions. Many couples are left with so many unmet needs and a lack of stability. My workaholism was my coping mechanism to avoid dealing with the reality of my world. The enemy always seeks to destroy what is precious to God and he hates anything that is good, sanctified, holy, or healthy in relationships and families.

This is why sexual addictions within a person is so strong and is not easily broken, until the *root cause* is dealt with. In this day and age, it runs rampid straight down to your average person, who you never would have thought was into this type of lifestyle. Sadly, many church leaders are heavily involved in pornography, infidelity, pride, along with having hard hearts all the while doing ministry.

Some of the horrible stories I have heard are of young children being molested by a Youth Minister or a Clergyman, (or woman), grooming them while they attended Church only to be lured into sexual abused later. Then there is the Sex Trafficking Industry and the realities of that type of abuse can leave one without any hope.

Yet, it is my prayer that what I have shared with you in this book will give some insight on how to get to the other side of abuse and addictions in your own life. My story is one that I did not want to write. I wish that my childhood and marriages could have been different and I have had to learn to mourn many things in my life. Abuse is a vicious cycle and, unless it is stopped, it *will* continue.

Learning from My Past

When I began to learn about Partner Betrayal Trauma, (PBT), I studied everything that I could get my hands on and it revolutionized my life. My inability to trust or remotely feel safe were *all* connected to the trauma I had experienced. It did not only come from my childhood abuse either or men, but from *every* dysfunctional relationship in my life.

I was programmed to be joined to men and women who were influenced by the enemy to destroy my destiny. This included my exs, family members, co-workers, and even those in the church, sadly. While my story, (and countless others), may be something that is becoming way too common these days, it does not have to all end poorly. I cannot say that it will be easy to recover from abuse, but it is absolutely *possible*.

There will need to be much re-training of the mind, will, and emotions – basically it is consistently re-programming one's brain. All the old dysfunction imprints have to be erased and that takes time. I chose to do it through my faith in God and by paying it forward in working with other women who are like me and you can to. Life *can* change. Healing *can* come. Restoration *can* happen. I have learned that, if I do my part, God will do His. It does not always turn out to be the way I want or when I want it, but true change does occur in time.

The key that I need to always remember is that I must keep my focus on changing *me*. This was all part of the decision to get healthy, which included getting medically treated for the issues I faced. Taking care of me for the first time in my life has been something to get adjusted to. God is continuing to redeem what the enemy has stolen and He is turning things around, (slowly, but surely), in my life.

Although I was raised in abuse, I never knew that I was in an abusive relationship, until I started to get healthy. Pursuing healthy boundaries, finding my voice, protecting myself, and staying true to my core values were all part of my re-training and deliverance. When one is in an abusive lifestyle, living in a healthy way is unheard of. You are taught to stay silent, pretend, deny, and make excuses for your abusers.

Another major part of my healing process was forgiving myself. That is the hardest thing for a victim of abuse to do, because we have been trained to take the blame for things. I was stripped of thinking for myself with the end result of me questioning everything, because of all my insecurities. Safety, trust, and love are foreign words in satan's world.

I have lived a shame-based mindset, which resulted in being emotionally unstable. My abuse numbed me from the reality that it *was not* healthy. It paralyzed me from thinking that I could have a happy life. I was programmed to endure my abuse, which only created a hardness about me.

Being spiritually abused by hose in the church came in the form of not being allowed to minister, because of my past. They lorded over me with their views of God and what love was, which really turned out to be distorted points of views. Jesus would *never* do to me what many religious people have done. Being taught to love our abusers in the church must come with balance. What is being shared to do in normal relationships *will not* work in abusive ones. It only fuels the addict/ abuser more to harm their victims.

Whenever I hear a woman minimize her situation, justify her abuser's ways, and deny that the problem is serious, I know she is living in abuse. When there is anxiety for your own safety, (or your children), that you avoid standing up for what is right, you are *definitely* in an abusive situation. When you cannot be yourself around certain individuals, there is *something* wrong. When you cannot go anywhere without another person giving you *permission* to do so or you fear more what others will think than what is best for you, there is a *problem*. When you are being forced to have sex, (whether married or not), you are being *raped*.

When you are silenced in having an opinion or need, you are being *verbally and emotionally* abused. When you have to ask for approval to buy things, are required to bring proof of store receipts, or are treated like a child with money, you are being *financially* abused. When Scripture is used to shame, control, or manipulate someone, you are being *spiritual* abused.

Abusers rule by fear, intimidation, control, and threats. They will do whatever they can to cut one off from anyone who could influence their victims from getting help. They are usually narcissistic, addicted to something, SRA victims, and highly traumatized in their own lives. The number one tool they use is to be charming and will try to woo their victims into a relationship. However, once they have them, their true colors come out.

I also had abusive relationships with women that were full of back biting, gossiping, and hypocrisy. Some of the worst experiences, (and the most painful), were the ones with women whom I confided in, especially at church. I have seen how women would take things shared with them in privacy and broadcasted it to others as, *"Prayer Requests."* Women can be addict/abusers to, so do not think that it is only limited to men.

If you have any of these issues with co-workers, family members, friends or acquaintances, it is time to re-evaluate your relationships more closely. If you do you see any of these signs, I urge you to get help right away. If not, you will be at the same place doing the same things 10-years from now. Life is way *too* short to live that way. You are worth so much more and deserve to have a life of being valued, respected, honored, and cherished. Then you can go out and do no less for others.

I highly recommend finding safe people to talk to or go to a Shelter for abused women. Do on-line searches for this type of information and read books on the very thing you are struggling with. There is so much free Christian materials out there and especially on YouTube. I did all these things and finally began breaking free little-by-little and you can too.

My Healing

When I began seeking help for myself, I felt led to start being vulnerable in telling my story. There are many women who are not able to share what they are going through, especially if they are being abused by their own husbands who hold high positions in the church.

Community, fellowship, and transparency in healthy relationships is why we were even created in the first place, because God longs to have that with each of us. He wants us to walk in healthy dynamics being able to love, (and be loved), the way He loves us through Jesus. I truly feel that everyone has a purpose in life. We were not put on this earth to just exist. We are all called to share the Gospel with others and to fulfill our God-given purposes.

Yet, because this thing we call, *"life,"* is so challenging, He has given us others to help us walk through things with. They may be friends, family, the Church, and those who are trained in various medical areas, but they need to be safe. I was determined to learn new ways to help myself become, *"unstuck,"* and go forward by have mature voices speaking into me.

I researched, the, *"Why behind my what."* What was the, *"why,"* behind, *"what,"* I was doing with my pain and healing? I soon learned the answer to this question. It was the negative imprints of the abuse in my past. This came in the form of suppressed childhood trauma, deep soul wounds, and demonic soul ties the enemy had me entangled in.

That was a lot of unpacking to do in getting me to a place of healing in all these areas. It has taken lots of time and energy, soul searching, journaling, and transparency with my story. Having been married more than once is not accepted that easily within organized religion and I have felt unloved in many ways.

Yet, God was faithful in leading me to the right places I needed to go to have caring relationships. As I became more honest with myself and others, I began to the feel shackles of abuse being broken off of me.

I no longer had to be, *"Ms. Perfect,"* and having all the answers. I am still learning today that I can be free to be me, even if it is at times a HOT MESS! When we wear masks to cover up things, we may fool others, but we are not fooling God. He wants us to be delivered from ourselves more than we do.

I have felt like there was a hole in my heart and this was why addict/abusers were able to get into a relationship with me. I was so love-starved that I had gravitated to men who were not good for me. I was attracted to what *I was* – broken. I needed to become well to be able to attract healthy men. One divorce is bad enough, but having gone through several was heart wrenching. There came a time when I finally had to face my truth – I was not going to be any good to God, myself, or others, unless I stopped long enough to face what my life really was.

It took me to a whole new level in feeling free. I was able to see God in a new way and I cried a lot, (still do). That was the sign that break through was happening, because I was taught *not* to cry. I fought doing so or showing too much emotion, because it only caused my addict/abusers to hurt me more. It meant that they had won in breaking me to the core of my being.

As a woman, (especially a Christian one), I felt that I needed to make my marriages work to validate who I was. Yes, I was mentally imbalanced, but I could not acknowledge that living in abuse contributed to me being *more* unstable. I deceived myself into thinking that God could heal my marriages and He could of. The problem was that it would take two willing individuals to do so. The men in my life were too sick themselves to see that they needed help.

I can honestly say that I have learned to see each of my exs differently now. I do not hate them anymore and I have forgiven them, even if it is by faith only. I have purposed to see them through God's eyes in being broken men in their hearts and souls. Each of them had their own set of demons to contend with and I have come to understand what all that means now.

As I have studied on numerous topics to heal, the lie that I am the only one who feels this way has disappeared. There are countless people who have gone through what I have and some have endured far worse abuse. Yet, the ultimate truth I know to be so is that God loves them, (and me), no matter what.

The devil is real and he truly does seek to kill, steal, and destroy. My purpose now is to fight the Good Fight of Faith and stay true to my own convictions in what God has called me to do. I can learn from my past, but I cannot stay stuck there anymore. I am not where I want to be, but I am not where I am going to be either. As time goes on, I want to learn from my pasts to lead me into a new tomorrow.

My Redemption

In my earlier years, I never thought I would be here today. I truly wanted to die and struggled with the thoughts of suicide regularly, which is draining on one's soul. Anyone who has dealt with depression knows what I am talking about. Thankfully, I am learning to accept that my past was not all my fault.

I have begun to accept who I am, (flaws and all), even when others do not. The truths that I embraced before are being replaced with God's truths for me and my life. Despite all the hate I have been subjected to, I still believe in, *"Love."* Why? Because God is teaching me that it is real in how He is using Jesus, (and others in my life), to love me past my pain.

As a woman, I am able to see things differently for myself in having a healthy relationship with a man. I have realized that I *do* have so much to offer someone, especially since I have never been in a Covenant Marriage the way God calls a marriage to be. Living in abuse causes many to not ever reach their life callings, have dreams, or goals, especially in marriage. Yet, I believe that God can, (and will), redeem all that I have walked through.

Despite their identity being stripped away from them, abuse survivors have a story to tell. When the Holy Spirit began walking me through my suppressed memories, it was overwhelming. I began to connect with the love of Jesus and God the Father in a different way. It was like parts of me being melted away in how I was loved before. There were days where all I could do was sit in the presence of God to allow Him to subside my pain. It was in those Quiet Time that I was met with some form of direction, words of inspiration, or messages that confirmed what I needed to hear.

When I began to see the heart of God for me, it was not at all what I had been taught before. The redemption that Jesus had given me was beyond my comprehension and it still can be today. I have never been able to wrap my mind around Jesus' sacrificial love. However, I have learned much about it in seeing *The Chosen Series* produced by Dallas Jenkins that tells the story of Christ's life. It has really put me in touch with who He is as a man and as God's son.

I have began to see Him in a more intimate way, which has led me to have a better understanding with Him not only my Savior, but in all that He died to give me. Now, when I was triggered, I begin to invite Jesus into the wounded areas of my heart. He then leads me to apply biblical principles and reach out more for prayer.

Often times, I hear Him asking me, *"Will you trust Me?"* Then I remember something I have heard or seen about how He had to trust God to redeem the world through Him. Not an easy task when you are faced with being brutally tortured and crucified. In April, it is my yearly tradition to watch, *The Passion of the Christ,"* created by Mel Gibson. As I do, I am always left awe struck at the depiction of Jesus laying down His life for mankind. I can honestly say that I if did not have my faith, my story would be a different one today.

What Is Your Story?

This is a question that many living in abuse do not like to look at, because it will require them to *deal* with suppressed pain. I lived there for longer than I should have. Eventually, it forced me to have those difficult conversations that needed to be had with myself and others in order for closure to come in my life on various things. At other times, it caused me to face the reality that I needed to leave a very toxic relationship.

I will be honest with you that there were areas in my life that got worse before getting better. It was a time of deep soul searching and lots reality checks. Then there was the grieving and mourning of what once was, even if it was a dysfunctional relationship.

One of the lies the enemy uses against women living in abuse is, *"It is not that bad. You are over reacting. You need to love unconditionally."* I am here to shout from the mountain tops, *"THOSE ARE ALL LIES!!!"* We were created for so much more and the quicker we accept that, the better off our lives will be.

Our identities are based on what *He says* we are not how long we have been married, the amount of children or grandchildren we have, what type of dog we own, if we have a vacation home, what brand of style we wear, and do we drive a top-of the line car. We have been brain-washed into believing that this is what matters and it *does not* in God.

Our lives cannot be defined by exterior things, fears, doubts, and unbelief, as mine was once. I believe that we are all gifted with things to do to help others and that we each have heavenly books written about the choices we make in this life. There is so much more to the Spiritual Realm than many realize. Some will be surprised on who is in Heaven when they arrive.

Our lives all depend on the daily choices we make here on earth. I have chosen to define my destiny not through being abused, but in how I daily choose to overcome being *freed* from living in abuse. I have often heard that the very areas of struggle one faces are what their callings are in. If one is an addict, they will minister to other addicts, etc., so what is it in your life that is your, *"thorn in the flesh?"* If you start there, you will quickly learn what your calling is. I never thought mine would be to help other women heal from abuse. In the midst of my own trauma, I could not remotely see how God would use it, but He has.

The other thing to determine what your story is will be to take an inventory on your life and pray into it. Journal as much as you can and then re-read your journals, asking for God's discernment. If you have dreams, write them down, and research what they mean by using a Biblical Dream Interpretation Book.

When tragedy strikes, many want to blame God for it, but they forget there is a devil and others who have free-will. We literally have the God-given right to reject all that He gave us through Jesus, if we want to. However, that would also mean that we would not have the gift of eternal life with Him in heaven. Here is a prayer that helps me when I awake:

"Good morning, Lord God, here I am ready to be filled afresh with your Dunamis Power. I want to carry this anointing everywhere I go, so that whoever I meet today will not just see me. I pray that they would be able to feel Your presence and will sense You all around me. May they encounter You, who is within me. May they recognize Your truth and love in everything I do. May they feel Your presence in all You do through me. May they feel you in my spirit, as your miracle-working power being released in them, in Jesus Name. Amen."

I encourage you to begin each day with inviting God into it. Have conversations with Jesus and ask the Holy Spirit to guide you in all you do. When you have a bad day or some triggers are set of, reach out to those who are safe that can walk it through with you. Just keep going forward at all costs. It is there that you will eventually find yourself and God. Lastly, always remember to, *"Take care of you…"*

Author Page

GYASMIN E. MATOS, is a Writer that will touch your heart and soul through sharing her Life Story. In, **GOD DOESN'T WASTE A HURT – A Life of Abuse to A Story of Redemption**, you will read about one woman's Journey of Healing from abusive relationships, being a survivor of Satanic Ritual Abuse, (SRA), and having victory in the midst of losing everything several times.

Coming from a background of living through various types of abuses has given Gyasmin the ability to understand those who thought they could never truly heal from the traumas of their pasts. Through it all, she has been broken with the things that break the heart of God making her who she is today. This book will help readers see that in the midst of this thing called, *"life,"* God Never Wastes A Hurt, (GDWAH).

Gyasmin writes about how God took her through not knowing who she really was to embracing who He had call her to be and how she became, *"unstuck,"* in her own Life Journey. The details shared will help a reader to see that everyone can overcome their battles, as she did. Through her faith, a willingness to change, and a heart for the things of God, He led her into her, *"Promise Land."*

You can find more information on Gyasmin and her writings by searching on-line for *"GDWAH."*

Printed in the United States
by Baker & Taylor Publisher Services